The Worldwide Hot Sauce Cookbook

150 Easy & Fiery Recipes from All Over the World
Selected Only for True Spicy Lovers

Brigham Mack

Table of Contents

Introduction

Chili is the main ingredient in hot sauce. This family of peppers, which includes well-known species like the cayenne and jalapeno, is native to Mexico. Like many other foods, it was introduced to international trade in the 14th century. Countless of the hot sauces we are familiar with today is a result of what humans have achieved with these exotic and novel chilies incorporated into their individual kitchens. Pepper and its production (fresh, roasted or fermented), additional herbs and spices, and viscosity, which can range from a paste to a smooth, pourable texture, affect the recipe. This is your complete guide to the hot sauce, where you can learn about the origins of many popular varieties and how they are made.

For decades, hot sauce has been a staple in the kitchen. However, most of us stick to the same old recipes and brands. This cookbook will help you discover some of the best hot sauce recipes from around the world.

We also provide you with useful information about the history of hot sauce, how to make your own, and where you can get some of the best sauces in the world.

If you're a salsa connoisseur or if you simply enjoy spicy food, then this cookbook is for you.

The recipes featured in this book will make it easy to add a spicy kick to any dish that could use a touch of flavor.

This book is a great resource for anyone who wants to learn more about hot sauce. The recipes are easy to follow, and the book is a great addition to any kitchen.

If you love hot sauce and are looking for some new recipes to try, this book is the perfect place to start. The recipes come from all over the world, so there's sure to be something that appeals to everyone. With helpful tips on how to make your own hot sauce at home as well as interesting facts about each recipe that will keep you entertained while cooking up a storm in the kitchen!

Chapter 1
Historical Background on Hot Sauce

History Of Hot Sauce

According to most sources, hot sauce is an ancient innovation that dates back to Mayan times. The early hot sauces were probably just a combination of peppers and water, but it wasn't long before people started growing pepper plants to produce as many as possible desired qualities in your peppers. Then, as with other dishes, colonialism led to the further development of the hot sauce by introducing components from other regions of the world, such as vinegar and various spices. It didn't take long for the spicy flavours to spread in the 19th century; the Tabasco company brought hot sauces into the commercial arena by bottling and marketing their products primarily to hotels and restaurants. Today there are several variations of hot sauce, from sriracha to buffalo sauce.

What Is Hot Made Of?

Most hot sauces are made with a mixture of chili peppers, vinegar, and salt. Fermentation is used in many hot sauces to give them an original flavour accent. They can be green, red, or even brown and can be liquid or pasty. While there are other hot condiments that don't contain chili peppers (mustard sauce, wasabi, horseradish), we're only looking at chili-based sauces.

What Makes Hot Sauce Hot?

Capsaicin is the molecule that gives peppers their unique pungent flavour (which also contributes to jalapeño hands). According to sources, capsaicin was naturally engineered to deter many animals from eating peppers, but the chemical has the opposite effect on a human. ...causing them to enjoy a pungent taste (warm food tastes good). An interesting fact to note is that the majority of bird species are unable to detect the strong flavor of capsaicin. This is thought to be an adaptation to facilitate the dissemination of the seeds of pepper plants, as the birds consume and subsequently excrete the seeds.

Chapter 2
Homemade Hot Sauce

Making Hot Sauce Step-by-Step

It's time to break down how to make the spicy sauce at home. We'll review some fundamentals that apply to most of the recipes in this book. Although most of the recipes are not fermented, we'll concentrate on the fermentation process because it's the hardest sort of sauce—non-fermented hot sauces are made primarily by "using a blender and avoiding touching your eye shortly after touching a pepper." I have faith in you! With this foundation, you'll be more than prepared to tackle a real sauce.

Keeping It Simple

The basic components of spicy sauce are simple. Most spicy sauces are prepared by combining a variety of the same basic components. As you can see, this results in a pretty forgiving procedure. Nonetheless, let us go through each step in further detail. Keep in mind that each recipe will include more explicit instructions.

Safety First

The capsaicin in chili peppers can burn not only your lips but also your hands and eyes. Plan to make lots of hot sauce. Investing in safety goggles and special gloves, whether pepper-specific gloves or disposable gloves, can be worthwhile to protect them. The same applies to working with chilies. Pouring cold milk over the area can be very beneficial if you have a burning sensation on your skin or in your eyes. Capsaicin is fat-soluble and is broken down more quickly in dairy products than in water. Depending on how hot the peppers are, it may take some time for the stinging to go away with or without milk. If you are ever concerned for any reason, do not hesitate to consult a doctor.

Step 1: Prepare the peppers

Preparing peppers requires a high-quality, sturdy chopping board and a sharp knife. To prepare fresh chiles, remove and discard the stems from the peppers, and Paprika can be prepared as indicated in the recipes. Reduce the heat to low, then slice the chiles vertically, scrape out the pith (the fluffy white part of the pepper) with a knife, discard the seeds, and rinse under running water. If you want to try growing your own chili peppers, remember that both fresh and dried chili seeds can be saved for future use.

Step 2: Pack The Jars

There are two basic fermentation processes used in fermented hot sauces: dry brine and wet brine. Dry salting involves combining vegetables with salt to extract a natural brine, and there are no traditional examples in this book. The process involves making a brine by combining salt and water and then pouring it over the fermented materials.

Please note that the lower levels of chlorine in regular tap water can affect the fermentation process. Purified water with household filter devices as well as purchased spring water, is usually sufficient.

Additionally, you should also use non-iodized table salt, as iodine inhibits the fermentation process. With any malolactic fermentation, you must keep the components below the brine level, which means they must remain buried in the brine. Ferment weights to help keep components submerged or use a cartridge (a parchment paper or cabbage leaf cover) to reduce oxygen exposure in pasty ferments. In certain cases, it will be practically difficult to keep everything under the brine at all times (think very small peppers and spices). In this situation, all you have to worry about is keeping the oxygen out and maintaining the ferment regularly by shaking and tapping the jar to avoid prolonged exposure of the components to the oxygen.

Step 3: Monitor The Progress

During fermentation, you'll most probably observe bubbles rising withinside the ferment. These bubbles are created through gases emitted by microorganisms as they spoil down glucose withinside the produce, and they may be a normal byproduct of fermentation. To maintain the jar from swelling and possibly shattering or spilling, "burp" it as soon as an afternoon through establishing it. However, maintain in thoughts that sure ferments create little or no effervescent motion at all, even as they may be fermenting very well. Here are some greater strategies to make sure that your highly spiced sauce is fermenting properly: When tasting, search for a sour, vinegar-like smell, murky brine, and/or acidic taste or effervescence at the tongue. At any time throughout the fermenting system, you could competently pattern your ferment. This is an awesome technique to analyze extra approximately the system and the way it alters the substances a little bit. If you're sure that fermentation isn't taking place, take into account transferring the ferment to a hotter location. Stop the fermentation and start over if you notice anything strange when it comes to sight, smell, or flavor.

Step 4: Strain And Mix

You can observe the steps in every fermented warm sauce recipe. However, in maximum cases, you may drain the ferment, after which you integrate it with different components earlier than mixing to provide a warm sauce. In sure circumstances, you may reserve a number of the brine you press if you want to offer extra flavor and probiotics. Most highly spiced sauces may be saved withinside the equal jar wherein they had been fermented. If you intend on growing a variety of warm sauces, it can be profitable to spend money on a few warm sauce bottles for that conventional warm sauce feel. Fermented, highly spiced sauces may be preserved withinside the fridge for as much as a year. Fermented ingredients are very acidic with the aid of using nature, making them perfect for preservation. The non-fermented, highly spiced sauce will maintain withinside the fridge for some weeks.

Troubleshooting

Even though fermentation is a rather simple and forgiving process, you're certain to have some questions.

Equipment Essentials

You'll need a few tools before digging into the recipes in this book. Don't worry, many of these are undoubtedly already in your kitchen. More specialist tools may be easily ordered and should not be prohibitively expensive.

A sharp knife, such as a chef's knife, is ideal for chopping.

A solid, durable cutting board is required for preparation. My personal favorites are bamboo and maple cutting blocks, which I appreciate the feel of and find easy to clean.

Working with peppers may be a fiery business, so wear gloves. Use disposable or pepper-specific cooking gloves to protect your hands from the capsaicin found in peppers.

A little metal or plastic funnel can come in helpful for bottling and storing your homemade spicy sauce.

Many of the recipes in this book call for the use of a food processor or blender to combine raw or cooked ingredients into a smooth sauce.

To separate solids from liquids in some recipes, particularly fermented ones, a strainer is required. I recommend a fine-mesh strainer with a tiny opening.

Certain recipes will instruct you to pan-fry some of the ingredients. A sturdy nonstick skillet would suffice.

In some recipes, the ingredients are boiled or cooked in a medium pot. A heavy-bottomed, sturdy cooking pot will suffice.

Some of the spicy sauce recipes and meals in this book will call for the use of a heavy-duty baking sheet to bake some of the components. A 9-by-13-inch sheet of paper will be sufficient.

Mason jars with lids: Mason jars with lids are useful for storing or fermenting hot sauce. For these recipes, I use 32-ounce wide-mouth mason jars.

Nice-to-Haves

Although the products mentioned below aren't strictly required, they can make your hot sauce trip a little smoother.

Hot sauce bottles are useful if you want to offer a friend or loved one some hot sauce as a present or if you just want to have the traditional hot sauce sensation yourself. They are widely available for buying online.

Fermentation weights: If you're new to fermentation and want to attempt some of the fermented hot sauces in this book, fermentation weights can make the process easier and more foolproof.

The weights keep your veggies immersed in brine, thus preventing them from spoiling. Simple glass weights that are made to suit most mason jars work well.

If you're pressed for time, a veggie chopper may make chopping produce a snap. It's a handy gadget that chops chiles and other vegetables all at once with the press of a lid or button.

Mandoline: This portable slicing utensil features razor-sharp blades. I find that mandoline comes in handy when it comes to rapidly and effectively slicing materials.

Grater: A little metal hand grater can help you mince garlic and ginger or zest citrus.

pH strips: For the fermented hot sauces in this book, pH strips might be a simple way to test and ensure that fermentation has happened appropriately. The pH of the finished fermented hot sauce should be 7 of 4.6 or less. If it's any higher, fermentation was most certainly a failure.

Pantry Essentials

Although fresh chiles and other vegetables are essential for producing hot sauce at home, the following pantry staples will be just as useful as you work your way through the recipes in this book.

Vinegar: Several vinegars will be used in this book, but you can normally swap any vinegar for another if necessary. Most spicy sauce recipes, whether store-bought or from this book, use vinegar.

Regular and non-iodized salt: Regular salt is necessary for bringing out the tastes in hot sauce, whilst non-iodized salt is required for fermenting hot sauces.

Dried spices and herbs: A wide range of dried spices and herbs are used to flavor the spicy sauces in this book. But it never hurts to be well-stocked in this department.

Granulated sugar is required as a sweetener in several of the recipes in this book.

As needed, different granulated sugars can be used interchangeably. White cane sugar, brown sugar, and coconut sugar are all acceptable options.

Bottled lemon and lime juice: Bottled lemon and lime juice are almost as good as fresh-squeezed juice and are useful for several of the recipes in this book.

Many spicy sauces will require the use of oil. Olive, grapeseed, and avocado oils are all beneficial to keep on hand.

Tomato paste: Some recipes call for a robust tomato flavor of tomato paste. Tomato paste is available in cans, jars, and tubes; any of these will suffice.

Tips For Making A Great Hot Sauce

The world is filled with wonderful hot sauces, but it can be near impossible to make a great one. If you're interested in perfecting your own hot sauce, here are some tips to consider:

Start with quality ingredients. Begin by finding a reputable local grocery store that carries fresh garlic and other seasonings that will enhance the quality of your finished product. When possible, you should also purchase fresh peppers (jalapenos, serranos) or dried chili flakes to ensure the best flavor profile.

Don't rush. It can be difficult to wait for your peppers to ripen and for the flavors of the garlic and seasonings to develop, but it will result in a better-finished product. Use a slow cooker or crock pot, which provides a steady temperature that prevents burning and ensures less risk of spoilage.

Use the right equipment. A stainless-steel saucepan is preferable over aluminum, which allows the flavors of your ingredients to mix well and develop in step with each other while also preventing scorching. You should also use a fine mesh strainer or cheesecloth to avoid losing valuable spices and seasonings in the bottom of your saucepan.

Experiment with different combinations of ingredients. Hot sauce recipes can vary greatly, and if you don't know what works best for your palate, you may end up with an over-the-top product that doesn't suit your needs. Experiment with different hot peppers, garlic varieties, spices, vinegar and salt to find the perfect combination for your palate.

Don't forget about the garnish. A great hot sauce doesn't have to taste good on its own; it can be great as a dip for tortilla chips or as a topping on tacos or grilled meats, or vegetables. Consider adding a touch of something sweet to balance the hot, acidic flavors.

Store and use up. Once you've made your sauce, let it sit for at least a month before using it. After that time, you can gradually reduce the pepper's heat level by soaking it in water or vinegar (or even vanilla extract) and blending it with other ingredients to make a less spicy sauce. You can also freeze unused batches of hot sauce in plastic containers or jar lids for safe storage until you need them.

Think outside the bottle. Use the hot sauce as a condiment; put it on eggs, grilled meat, tofu, sandwiches and more. You can even use it to season soups, salsa or stews for a unique taste the next time you make them.

Experiment with extracts. While you may not always want to add hot sauces to your favorite recipes, vanilla extract is an excellent enhancer of hot sauce and can be used to add a unique flavor without adding heat. You can create much better sauces by using extracts than plain vinegar or lemon juice.

Try different combinations of fruit and spices. While many hot sauces tend to taste like chile peppers, especially as they are heated, they can also be complemented with other ingredients such as dried fruit or vanilla. You can also add fresh spices such as cinnamon or nutmeg to your sauces to add a new flavor.

Chill it if you want to bring out the heat. If you would like to consume a milder sauce, chill it before serving by placing the container in the refrigerator until you're ready for a cold meal. You can even let the sauce sit on an ice bath (freezing ice cubes in water) for several hours and then reheat it on the stove.

Go "all natural. " If you're interested in making a healthier, all-natural hot sauce, skip the sugar and processed ingredients; instead, try mixing hot peppers with fresh fruit such as apples and bananas. You can also try mixing your hot sauce with vinegar or lemon juice for a fresher taste.

Use the hot sauce as an ingredient in other dishes. Not only can you use sauces on their own as a dip or topping, but they can also be used as a flavoring agent in meals such as soups, stews and burgers. Try using a mixture of spicy ingredients for seasoning the meat before cooking it.

Chapter 3
Worldwide Recipes

3.1: American Hot Sauce Recipes

Texas-Style Picante Sauce

Prep time: 10 minutes | Cook time: 30 minutes | Makes 35 ounces

Ingredients:

- 7 halved standard size Roma tomatoes
- 6 stemmed fresh jalapenos
- 1 bell pepper, halved and stemmed
- 1 sliced white or yellow onion
- 1 cup distilled white vinegar
- ¼ cup granulated sugar
- 5 garlic cloves, peeled
- two tbsp tomato paste
- 2 tsp sea salt
- 1 teaspoon cumin powder
- ⅛ tsp fresh ground black pepper

Directions:

1. Combine the tomatoes, peppers, onion, vinegar, garlic, sugar, tomato paste, salt, cumin, and pepper in a food processor or blender. Blend until well combined but slightly chunky.
2. Bring the blended ingredients to a boil in a large pot over high heat. Reduce the heat to medium-low and cover for 25 to 30 minutes. Remove from the heat and set aside to cool to room temperature.
3. Keep refrigerated for up to 8-10 days.

Per Serving:

Calories: 47| Fat: 1g| Carbs: 16g| Sodium: 152mg

☆ ☆ ☆ ☆ ☆

Louisiana Pepper Sauce

Prep time: 10 minutes | Cook time: 5 minutes | Makes 20 ounces

Ingredients:

- 1 pound stemmed fresh red jalapenos (about 7 peppers)
- 2 cups vinegar, white
- 2 tsp. salt

Directions:

1. Combine the jalapeños, vinegar, and salt in a large pot over high heat. Continue cooking, then lower to medium heat for 6 minutes or until the chiles are tender.
2. Place the jalapeños mixture in a blender or food processor and blend until smooth, leaving a vent for steam to escape. Allow cooling to room temperature.
3. Refrigerate the mixture for 1 to 2 weeks before using it in an airtight container.
4. Keep refrigerated for up to 4 months.

Per Serving:

Calories: 0g| Fat: 0g| Carbs: 1g| Sodium: 1075mg

☆ ☆ ☆ ☆ ☆

New Mexican–Style Hatch Green Chile Hot Sauce

Prep time: 5-10 minutes | Cook time: 5-10 minutes | Makes 20 ounces

Ingredients:

- 1 tablespoon extra-virgin olive oil
- 1 cup fresh cilantro, chopped
- 1 white onion, diced
- 8 garlic cloves, minced
- 1 cup peeled, stemmed, and chopped roasted Hatch green chiles
- ½ teaspoon ground cumin
- ¼ teaspoon ground oregano
- ¼ cup lime juice
- ¼ cup honey
- 1 teaspoon sea salt

Directions:

1. In a food processor or blender, combine cooked onions and garlic with chile, coriander, cumin, oregano, lime juice, honey, and salt. Heat the oil in a frying pan over medium heat until it reaches the desired temperature. Then, add the onions and garlic and thoroughly mix the ingredients. It can be stored in the refrigerator for 8-10 days.

Per Serving:

Calories: 68| Fat: 0g| Carbs: 5g| Sodium: 162mg

☆ ☆ ☆ ☆ ☆

Fermented Buffalo Sauce

Makes 20 ounces | Prep time: 12 minutes | Fermentation time: 6 to 7 days

Ingredients:

- 15-pound stemmed fresh cayenne or Tabasco peppers (about 15 peppers)
- 1½ peeled garlic clove
- 2½ cups unchlorinated water
- 2 tbsp non-iodized sea salt
- 14 cups of white vinegar
- ¼ cup melted salted butter
- ¼ tsp smoked paprika

Directions:

1. Mix chilies and garlic in a clean container with water and salt to make a brine, then pour it into a jar of vegetable juice. Store at room temperature, out of direct sunlight, with the lid tightly closed, tapping daily for 5 to 6 days.
2. Mix together the leaven, vinegar, butter, and paprika in a food processor or blender to create a paste for this recipe.
3. It can be stored in the refrigerator for up to 10 months.

Per Serving:

Calories: 68| Fat: 0g| Carbs: 5g| Sodium: 162mg

☆ ☆ ☆ ☆ ☆

Jalapeno Ranch Sauce

Makes 6-8 Servings | Cooking + Prep Time: 15 minutes

Ingredients:

- 11/2 cup plain Greek yogurt
- 1/2 cup olive oil
- 1 tablespoon white vinegar
- 1 1/4 clove garlic
- 2 jalapeño pepper, ribbed and seeded
- 1/2 cup fresh parsley
- 1 tbsp freeze-dried dill
- 1/2 teaspoon onion powder
- 1 teaspoon coarse salt

Directions:

1. Blend all ingredients together in a food processor till creamy and smooth.
2. Serve over salad or other entrée or side dish.

Per Serving:

Calories: 181| Fat: 15g| Carbs: 11.7g| Sodium: 6.2g

☆ ☆ ☆ ☆ ☆

New Mexican Red Sauce

Prep time: 15 minutes | Cook time: 20-25 minutes | Makes 20 ounces

Ingredients:

- 1.5 ounces dried New Mexico red chiles (sometimes called red Hatch chiles), stemmed (about 12 chiles)
- 2 cups water
- 1 teaspoon salt
- 1 tablespoon all-purpose flour
- 2 tablespoons avocado oil
- ½ teaspoon dried oregano
- ½ teaspoon garlic powder
- ½ teaspoon ground cumin

Directions:

2. Mix the chiles, water and salt in a saucepan over high heat; bring to a boil, then lower to a simmer. Cook for 10 minutes, or until chiles are soft and tender, then add them to a blender or food processor. Blend until smooth, allowing steam to escape through a vent, then strain the mixture through a fine-mesh strainer.
3. Over high heat, heat a medium skillet. In a skillet, combine the flour and oil by gently stirring. Oregano, garlic powder, cumin, and strained chile puree should be included. Approximately 10 minutes, stirring frequently, cook until thick.
4. You can use the sauce right away or let it cool to room temperature before storing it in the refrigerator for up to a week.

Per Serving:

Calories: 123| Fat: 1g| Carbs: 56g| Sodium: 654mg

☆ ☆ ☆ ☆ ☆

Spicy Southern-Style Barbecue Sauce

Prep time: 7 minutes | Cook time: 37 minutes | Makes 35 ounces

Ingredients:

- 1 tablespoon olive oil
- ½ yellow onion, chopped
- 5 garlic cloves, minced
- 2 Carolina Reaper chiles, stemmed and minced
- 3 cups ketchup
- 1 cup apple cider vinegar
- ¾ cup granulated sugar
- ¼ cup honey
- 2 tablespoons Worcestershire sauce (vegetarian or nonvegetarian)
- 1 teaspoon salt
- ¼ teaspoon crushed red pepper flakes
- ¼ teaspoon celery seed

Directions:

1. Heat the oil, onion, garlic, and chiles in a medium saucepan over medium heat. Cook for 5 minutes or until the vegetables are softened.
2. Heat the ketchup, vinegar, sugar, honey, Worcestershire sauce, salt, crushed red pepper flakes, and celery seed in a large saucepan over high heat. Bring to a boil, then reduce to low heat. Simmer, stirring occasionally, for 30 minutes. Allow the sauce to cool for 10 minutes after it has been removed from the heat.
3. Place the sauce in a blender or food processor. Blend until smooth, allowing steam to escape if the mixture is still hot. Allow it to come to room temperature.
4. Keep refrigerated for up to a month.

Per Serving:

Calories: 30| Fat: 0g| Carbs: 11g| Sodium: 209mg

☆ ☆ ☆ ☆ ☆

Fermented Pebre

Prep time: 9 minutes | Fermentation time: 4-5 days | Makes 20 ounces

Ingredients:

- 4 Roma tomatoes, quartered
- ¾ cup chopped fresh cilantro
- 5 scallions, white and green parts, chopped
- 7 garlic cloves
- 1 aji amarillo or habanero, chopped
- 1 teaspoon non-iodized salt
- ¼ cup red wine vinegar
- 1 tablespoon olive oil

Directions:

1. Combine the tomatoes, cilantro, scallions, garlic, chile, and salt in a blender or food processor. Blend until just combined, leaving a few tomato chunks throughout.
2. Pour the mixture into a clean jar. Screw on the lid tightly and keep the jar at room temperature, away from direct sunlight, for 5 days, burping it daily.
3. When the fermentation process is finished, combine the contents of the jar with the vinegar and oil.
4. Keep refrigerated for up to 2 weeks.

Per Serving:

Calories: 188| Fat: 30g| Carbs: 11.8g| Sodium: 482mg

☆ ☆ ☆ ☆ ☆

Costa Rican–Style Hot Sauce

Prep time: 16 minutes | Makes 24 ounces

Ingredients:

- 2 ancho chiles, stemmed
- 1 cup baby carrots, halved
- 1 yellow onion, halved
- 2 garlic cloves
- 1 cup white vinegar
- ¼ cup granulated sugar
- 2 tablespoons blackstrap molasses
- 1 teaspoon ground yellow mustard
- ½ teaspoon celery seed
- 1½ teaspoons salt

Directions:

1. Cover the chiles in a small bowl with boiling water and set aside for 10 minutes or until soft.
2. Transfer the softened chiles to a blender or food processor. Combine the carrots, onion, garlic, vinegar, sugar, molasses, ground mustard, celery seed, and salt in a mixing bowl. Blend until completely smooth.
3. Keep refrigerated for up to 2 weeks.

Per Serving:

Calories: 200| Fat: 1g| Carbs: 20g| Sodium: 902mg

Hawaiian Chile Pepper Water

Prep time: 8 minutes | Cook time: 2-5 minutes | Makes 15 ounces

Ingredients:

- 7 fresh Hawaiian chiles or habanero peppers, stemmed and thinly sliced 1-inch knob of fresh ginger root, thinly sliced
- 4 garlic cloves, crushed
- 1 cup water
- 1½ teaspoons alaea salt or sea salt
- ½ cup white vinegar

Directions:

1. In a clean glass jar, combine the chiles, ginger, and garlic. Place aside.
2. Heat the water and salt in a small saucepan over high heat. Bring to a boil, then remove from the heat.
3. Pour the hot, salted water over the contents of the glass jar. Fill the jar halfway with vinegar. Allow it to cool to room temperature before sealing and storing it in the refrigerator.

Per Serving:

Calories: 112| Fat: 1g| Carbs: 5.7g| Sodium: 237mg

☆ ☆ ☆ ☆ ☆

Salsa Taquera

Prep time: 9-10 minutes | Cook time: 7 minutes | Makes 18 ounces

Ingredients:

- 1 tablespoon avocado oil
- 2 medium tomatoes, halved
- 3 medium tomatillos, husks removed
- 1 white onion, halved
- 0.5-ounce dried arbol chiles stemmed (about 18 chiles)
- 3 garlic cloves
- 1½ teaspoons salt

Directions:

1. Heat the oil, tomatoes, tomatillos, and onion in a large skillet over medium heat. Cook for 5 minutes, stirring frequently, or until the tomatoes begin to blister.
2. Place the mixture in a blender or food processor and set aside until the next step is completed.
3. Toast the dried chiles in the same skillet over medium heat for 2 minutes or until fragrant, flipping frequently to avoid burning.
4. Combine the toasted chiles with the remaining ingredients in a blender. Mix the garlic and salt in a bowl. Blend until smooth, leaving a vent open to let the steam escape. Allow it to come to room temperature.
5. Keep refrigerated for up to a week.

Per Serving:

Calories: 10g| Fat: 5g| Carbs: 2.7g| Sodium: 102mg

☆ ☆ ☆ ☆ ☆

Smooth Salsa Verde

Prep time: 6 minutes | Cook time: 12 minutes | Makes 19 ounces

Ingredients:

- 1-pound tomatillos, husks removed
- 2 serrano peppers, stemmed
- 2 jalapeños, stemmed
- 2 garlic cloves, peeled
- ½ cup chopped fresh cilantro
- ½ teaspoon salt

Directions:

1. Cover the tomatillos with cold water in a medium saucepan over medium heat and bring to a simmer.
2. Simmer for 10 minutes or until the tomatillos are soft but not mushy. Tomatillos should be drained.
3. Combine the tomatillos, chiles, garlic, cilantro, and salt in a blender or food processor. Blend until smooth, leaving a vent open to let the steam escape. Allow it to come to room temperature.
4. Keep refrigerated for up to a week.

Per Serving:

Calories: 1 | Fat: 2g | Carbs: 0g | Sodium: 272mg

☆ ☆ ☆ ☆ ☆

Pico de Gallo

Prep time: 10 minutes | Makes 28 ounces

Ingredients:

- 4 medium tomatoes, chopped
- 1 white onion, chopped
- 4 jalapeño, stemmed and minced
- 1 garlic clove, minced
- ¾ cup chopped fresh cilantro
- 2 tablespoons freshly squeezed lime juice
- ½ teaspoon salt

Directions:

1. Toss the tomatoes, onion, jalapeño, garlic, cilantro, lime juice, and salt in a medium mixing bowl to coat.
2. Keep refrigerated for up to a week.

Per Serving:

Calories: 1| Fat: 0g| Carbs: 1.7g| Sodium: 750g

☆ ☆ ☆ ☆ ☆

Smooth Salsa Verde

Prep time: 7 minutes | Cook time: 12 minutes | Makes 16 ounces

Ingredients:

- 1 lb. red chilies, heads removed
- 4 large red bell peppers, deseeded and chopped
- 4 garlic cloves, chopped
- ¼ cup chopped fresh basil
- ½ cup chopped fresh cilantro
- 1 tsp smoked Paprika
- ½ cup vegetable oil
- 1 lemon, juiced
- Salt to taste

Directions:

1. Combine all of the ingredients in a blender and process until mostly smooth.
2. Pour sauce into an airtight jar and refrigerate until ready to use.

Per Serving:

Calories: 2| Fat: 5g| Carbs: 2g| Sodium: 702mg

☆ ☆ ☆ ☆ ☆

New Mexican Red Sauce

Prep time: 9 minutes | Cook time: 22 minutes | Makes 25 ounces

Ingredients:

- 1.5 ounces dried New Mexico red chiles (sometimes called red Hatch chiles), stemmed (about 18 chiles)
- 2 cups water
- 1 teaspoon salt
- 1 tablespoon all-purpose flour
- 2 tablespoons avocado oil
- ½ teaspoon dried oregano
- ½ teaspoon garlic powder
- ½ teaspoon ground cumin

Directions:

1. In a large pot of boiling water, combine the chilies and salt. Bring to a boil, then turn down to a low setting. Cook for 10 minutes or until the chiles are soft and plump. Blend them in a food processor until smooth, with a vent open to allow steam to escape.
2. Melt the butter in a medium skillet over high heat. Combine the strained chile puree, oregano, garlic powder, and cumin in a mixing bowl. In the same bowl, combine the flour and oil until smooth. Cook until thickened, about 10 minutes, stirring frequently.
3. Use immediately or cool to room temperature before storing in the refrigerator for up to 1 week.

Per Serving:

Calories: 60| Fat: 0g| Carbs: 4g| Sodium: 132mg

☆ ☆ ☆ ☆ ☆

Jerk Sauce

Prep time: 8 minutes | Makes 28 ounces

Ingredients:

- 2-ounce fresh Scotch bonnets or habaneros stemmed (about 10 peppers)
- 2 yellow onions, halved
- 3 scallions, white and green parts, halved
- 6 garlic cloves
- 1-inch knob of fresh ginger root, peeled
- 7 sprigs of fresh thyme
- 1 tablespoon allspice berries (about 30 berries)
- ¾ cup orange juice
- ¼ cup soy sauce or coconut aminos
- ¼ cup lime juice
- 2 tablespoons granulated sugar
- 1 teaspoon freshly ground black pepper
- 1 teaspoon salt

Directions:

1. In a blender or food processor, combine the peppers, onion, scallions, garlic, ginger, thyme, allspice, orange juice, coconut aminos, lime juice, sugar, black pepper, and salt. Blend on high until totally smooth.
2. Refrigerate for up to ten days.

Per Serving:

Calories: 40| Fat: 0g| Carbs: 4g| Sodium: 270mg

☆ ☆ ☆ ☆ ☆

Jamaican Scotch Bonnet Pepper Sauce

Prep time: 10 minutes | Cook time: 25 minutes | Makes 16 ounces

Ingredients:

- 2 tablespoons avocado oil
- 1 yellow onion, chopped
- 6 carrots, chopped
- 2 chayotes, peeled, pitted, and chopped
- 10 allspice berries (about 1 teaspoon)
- 3 garlic cloves, peeled
- 1-inch knob of ginger, peeled and cut into ⅛-inch slices
- 8 Scotch bonnets or habaneros, stemmed and chopped
- ½ cup white vinegar

Directions:

1. Cook for approximately 10 minutes, stirring periodically, or until the onion softens. Add the carrots, allspice, garlic, and ginger to the pot of hot oil and heat over medium heat.
2. Cook for approximately 10 minutes, stirring periodically, or until the chili softens. In a food processor or blender, blend the cooked mixture with the oils and spices until smooth.
3. Using a fine-mesh strainer, sift the mixture, retaining the liquid and discarding the solids. Allow it to come to room temperature before using.
4. Store in the refrigerator for up to a month.

Per Serving:

Calories: 30| Fat: 15g| Carbs: 2g| Sodium: 380mg

☆ ☆ ☆ ☆ ☆

Hot Pepper Sauce

Serving: Yield: 1 cup | Preparation Time: 5 mins

Ingredients:

- 1/4 cup extra-virgin olive oil
- 1 small red onion, diced
- 1/2 tsp. cumin
- 1/8 tsp. cayenne
- Coarse sea salt
- 1 large clove of garlic, minced
- 1 habanero chile, minced
- 1/4 cup tomato paste
- 1/4 cup tomato sauce
- 2 tsp. apple cider vinegar
- 1/4 cup water
- 1/2 tsp. Freshly ground white pepper

Directions:

1. Warm the oil in a saucepan over low heat. Add half a teaspoon of salt, cayenne pepper, cumin, and onion. Cook for 8 minutes or until the onions start to caramelize.
2. Stir in the chile and garlic and cook for another 2 minutes. Fill the container halfway with water, vinegar, tomato sauce, and tomato paste. Stir thoroughly, then cook for 5-7 minutes or until it starts to thicken.
3. In an upright blender, combine all of the ingredients. Add in the white pepper and purée until smooth. Season with salt to taste. Refrigerate in a firmly sealed container.

Per Serving:

Calories: 304 | Carb: 14 g | Fat: 28 g | Fiber: 3 g | Protein: 3 g | Sodium: 413 mg

☆ ☆ ☆ ☆ ☆

Sos Ti-Malice

Prep time: 8 minutes | Cook time: 12 minutes | Makes 30 ounces

Ingredients:

- ½ cup olive oil
- 2 fresh Scotch bonnets or habaneros, stemmed and chopped
- 2 medium red bell pepper, chopped
- 3 medium green bell pepper, chopped
- 1 shallot, chopped
- 1 white onion, chopped
- 3 garlic cloves, peeled
- 4 sprigs of fresh thyme, stems removed
- 1 cup lime juice
- 3 tablespoons tomato paste
- 1 teaspoon salt

Directions:

1. In a large saucepan, heat the oil, chiles, bell peppers, shallot, onion, garlic, and thyme; leave over medium heat. Cook, stirring occasionally, for 5 minutes or until the veggies soften.
2. Combine the lime juice, tomato paste, and salt in a mixing bowl. After completely combining, bring to a simmer. Take the pan off the heat.
3. Cool to room temperature before using or keeping in the refrigerator for up to 10 days.

Per Serving:

Calories: 98 | Fat: 0g| Carbs: 4g| Sodium: 742g

☆ ☆ ☆ ☆ ☆

Hawaiian Chile Pepper Water

Prep time: 5 minutes | Cook time: 1 minute | Makes 20 ounces

Ingredients:

- 8 fresh Hawaiian chiles or habanero peppers, stemmed and thinly sliced 1-inch knob of fresh ginger root, thinly sliced
- 4 garlic cloves, crushed
- 1 cup water
- 1½ teaspoons alaea salt or sea salt
- ½ cup white vinegar

Directions:

1. Combine the chilies, ginger, and garlic in a clean glass jar. Set aside.
2. In a small saucepan, boil the water and salt over high heat. Bring to a boil, then turn off the heat.
3. Fill the glass jar halfway with boiling salted water. Half-fill the container with vinegar. Allow it to cool to room temperature before closing and refrigerating.

Per Serving:

Calories: 77 | Fat: 1g| Carbs: 11g| Sodium: 632mg

☆ ☆ ☆ ☆ ☆

Mexican Hot Sauce

Serving Size: 10 | Preparation Time: 25 mins

Ingredients:

- 3 cups dried red chili peppers
- 1/2 seeds
- 1/4 cup onion flakes (dried)
- 1 tsp. salt
- 1 tsp. cumin powder
- 1 tsp. oregano
- 1 Tbsp. chili powder
- 1 tsp. paprika
- 4 Tbsp. white vinegar
- 2 cups water
- 16 oz. tomato sauce

Directions:

1. Melt the butter in the oven on high heat and bring it to a boil, then reduce to low heat and continue to cook for 10 minutes.
2. In a blender, combine the cooked mixture with tomato sauce.
3. Blend until completely smooth.
4. Refrigerate in a firmly sealed container.

Per Serving:

Calories: 125| Fat: 1g| Carbs: 1g| Sodium: 536mg

☆ ☆ ☆ ☆ ☆

Canned Mexican Hot Sauce

Serving Size: 12 cups | Preparation Time: 3 hrs

Ingredients:

- 5 lb. Roma tomatoes
- 2 sweet onions (large)
- 1 head garlic
- 10 jalapeno peppers
- 2 Tbsp. canning salt
- 2 Tbsp. granulated garlic
- 1/2 cup chopped cilantro

Directions:

1. In a food processor, finely crush the onions, half of the garlic, and half of the jalapenos. To create the sauce, strain the fresh romas through a victorio strainer.
2. In a large kettle, combine the sauce, ground onions, garlic, and jalapenos, as well as the salt and granulated garlic. Slowly simmer for 2 to 3 hours or until the sauce is quite thick.
3. Mince the remaining garlic and finely cut the remaining jalapenos. Just before processing, add them to the sauce, along with the fresh cilantro. I use half and full pints. It makes about 12 cups of sauce. Process in a water bath or steam canner according to the directions in the canning book.

Per Serving:

Calories: 130 Fat: 2g| Carbs: 1g| Sodium: 466mg

☆ ☆ ☆ ☆ ☆

Mexican Hot Sauce

Serving Size: 5 cups | Preparation Time: 10 mins

Ingredients:

- 18.5 oz. tomato juice
- 12.5 oz. tomato puree
- 15.5 oz. tomatoes (whole)
- 6 jalapeno peppers (pickled stems removed, such as Trappeys)
- 4 Tbsp. Tabasco Sauce
- 1/2 Tbsp. ground cumin
- 1 1/2 Tbsp. chili powder
- 3/4 Tbsp. garlic (minced)
- 1 1/2 Tbsp. white sugar
- 1/2 Tbsp. paprika
- 1 Tbsp. salt

Directions:

1. Fill the bottom of the blender or food processor with whole peppers and tomatoes.
2. Puree/chop the remaining ingredients till thick but not chunky.
3. Refrigerates for many weeks.

Per Serving:

Calories: 40| Fat: 1g| Carbs: 1g| Sodium: 325mg

☆ ☆ ☆ ☆ ☆

Homemade Hot Sauce

Prep time: 9 mins | Cook time: 25 mins | Serves: 4 cups

Ingredients:

- 5 whole tomatoes, halved
- 1-pound mixed spicy peppers
- 1 full garlic bulb, divided into cloves, olive oil drizzle
- 1 tablespoon sea salt
- 12 teaspoon apple cider vinegar
- 2 tbsp raw cane or palm sugar
- 12 cup water

Directions:

1. Preheat the oven to 350°F/175°C.
2. Mix together the chiles, tomatoes, roasted garlic and peeled roasted garlic in a blender or food processor to create a paste. Add apple cider vinegar, sugar, salt, and water and blend until completely smooth.
3. Add a bit extra water if you want a runnier sauce.
4. Refrigerates for roughly a month.

Per Serving:

Calories: 54| Fat: 1g| Carbs: 3g| Sodium: 532mg

☆ ☆ ☆ ☆ ☆

Red Harissa Sauce

Preparation Time: 10 mins | Cooking Time: 8 mins

Serving Size: 1 cup

Ingredients:

- 3 large red bell peppers
- 2 ½ tbsp. white wine vinegar
- 4 garlic cloves, crushed
- 2 Fresno chilies, heads removed, deseeded, chopped
- 1 tsp. cumin powder
- Salt and black pepper to taste
- ¼ cup extra-virgin olive oil

Directions:

1. Roast the peppers over an open flame, rotating frequently, until browned all over. Transfer to a bowl and set aside to cool.
2. Remove the seeds and place them in a food processor. Blend in the remaining ingredients until smooth.
3. Serve sauce immediately and store any leftovers in sealed jars in the refrigerator.

Per Serving:

Calories: 67| Fat: 6g| Carbs: 7g| Sodium: 340mg

☆ ☆ ☆ ☆ ☆

Joe's Soak Sauce

Preparation Time: 25 mins | Serving Size: 4 cups

Ingredients:

- 6 dried New Mexico red chiles
- 6 dried chipotle chiles
- 3 fresh habanero chiles, stemmed
- 6 medium garlic cloves, peeled
- ¼ cup coarsely chopped yellow onion
- 2 cups red wine vinegar
- ¼ cup bourbon
- ¼ cup freshly squeezed lemon juice
- ⅓ cup loosely packed fresh rosemary
- 1½ teaspoons sea salt

Directions:

1. Preheat the oven to 250 degrees Fahrenheit.
2. Roast the dried chiles on a baking sheet for 3 minutes or until they smell fragrant. Soak them in a saucepan of boiling water for 20 minutes or until soft. Combine all of the ingredients in a blender and mix for 3 minutes.
3. Fill the bottles with the mixture and seal them. This sauce improves with age and may be stored in the refrigerator for 6 weeks.

Per Serving:

Calories: 35| Fat: 1g| Carbs: 7g| Sodium: 265mg

☆ ☆ ☆ ☆ ☆

Peri Peri Sauce

Preparation Time: 6 mins | Serving Size: 6 cups

Ingredients:

- 1 lb. red chilies, heads removed
- 4 large red bell peppers, deseeded and chopped
- 4 garlic cloves, chopped
- ¼ cup chopped fresh basil
- ½ cup chopped fresh cilantro
- 1 tsp smoked Paprika
- ½ cup vegetable oil
- 1 lemon, juiced
- Salt to taste

Directions:

1. In a blender, combine all of the ingredients and pulse until almost smooth.
2. Refrigerate the sauce in an airtight container until ready to use.

Per Serving:

Calories: 27| Fat: 5g| Carbs: 4g| Sodium: 135g

☆ ☆ ☆ ☆ ☆

Inner Beauty Hot Sauce

Serving Size: 4 cups | Preparation Time: 5 mins

Ingredients:

- 4 cups fresh Scotch bonnet chiles, stemmed and chopped
- 1 cup ballpark-style yellow mustard
- 1 ripe mango, peeled, pitted, and chopped
- ½ cup freshly squeezed orange juice
- ¼ cup distilled white vinegar
- ¼ cup packed brown sugar
- 1 teaspoon curry powder
- 1 teaspoon ground cumin
- 1 teaspoon ground coriander
- Salt and freshly ground black pepper

Directions:

1. In a food processor, combine all of the ingredients and purée. Wear rubber gloves and a painter's mask while combining this many Scotch bonnets; the fumes will send you and your dog's running.
2. Fill bottles with the mixture and seal them. Refrigerate the sauce for up to 3 weeks.

Per Serving:

Calories: 67| Fat: 1g| Carbs: 6g| Sodium: 246mg

☆ ☆ ☆ ☆ ☆

Basic Brine Mash

Serving Size: 6 cups | Preparation Time: 10 mins

Ingredients:

- 1-2 cups brine (1-quart unchlorinated water + 3 tbsp salt)
- 4-6 ounces of dried chiles, enough to cram a pint jar securely

Directions:

1. Fill a narrow-mouthed pint jar halfway with chilies. Wedge them beneath the jar's shoulder to keep them immersed in the brine.
2. Pour in enough brine to thoroughly cover the chiles, pressing as you go to expel any air trapped inside the dried peppers. Screw the lid securely shut. (Keep any remaining brine in the refrigerator.) It will keep for one week; after that, trash it and start over.)
3. Place the jar on a platter and leave it to ferment for 2 to 3 weeks away from direct sunlight. As required, burp the ferment. Because some of the brine may bubble out, always open the jar over a plate. Top up with saved brine solution as required to keep the chiles covered.
4. The brine will turn orange and murky as it ferments. When it tastes acidic, you'll know it's done. Place the ingredients in a blender, brine and all, and puree until smooth.
5. Remove the seeds and skin using a sieve. The mash can be served as is or used to make a sauce.

Per Serving:

Calories: 67| Fat: 2g| Carbs: 9g| Sodium: 371mg

☆ ☆ ☆ ☆ ☆

Chipotle Salsa

Serving Size: 5 cups | Preparation Time: 5 mins

Ingredients:

- 3 cups chopped tomatoes
- 1 cup chopped fresh cilantro
- 3 tbsps. Fresh lime juice
- 2 tbsps. Chopped canned chipotle chilies in adobo sauce (sold at Latin American markets)
- 1 1/2 tsp. Ground cumin

Directions:

1. Combine all of the ingredients in a medium mixing basin. Season to taste with pepper and salt.

Per Serving:

Calories: 19| Carbs: 4 g| Fiber: 1 g| Protein: 1 g| Sodium: 47 mg

☆ ☆ ☆ ☆ ☆

Garlic Ancho Chile Jam

Serving Size: 5 cups | Preparation Time: 60 mins

Ingredients:

- 5 medium heads of garlic
- 5 tbsps. olive oil
- 3 tbsps. mild honey
- 5 oz. dried ancho chiles, stems, seeds, and veins
- 3 tbsps. cider vinegar

Directions:

2. Preheat the oven to 350 degrees Fahrenheit.
3. Wrap the heads in foil to keep them together and cook until they are just starting to soften, then add salt and pepper to taste. Bake for 40 minutes or until the potatoes are soft. Allow to cool until warm.
4. Soak the chilies in boiling water for 20 minutes, or until softened, before adding them to the oven-roasting pan with the garlic. Drain.
5. Squeeze the garlic from its skins and place it in a food processor; Purée the remaining 2 tablespoons of oil, honey, vinegar, chilies, and salt to taste. Purée should be forced into a basin using a sieve; use a hand blender to purée the mixture.

Per Serving:

Calories: 35| Fat: 0g| Carbs: 2g| Sodium: 480 mg

☆ ☆ ☆ ☆ ☆

Garlic And Achiote Fermented Hot Sauce

Preparation Time: 20 mins | Serving Size: 1 Jar

Ingredients:

- 2 garlic cloves & 1 cup olive oil
- 1 lb. fresh red chiles (such as cayenne, Fresno, or Holland), coarsely chopped
- 3 tbsps. kosher salt & 3 tbsps. sugar
- 3 tbsps. achiote (annatto) seeds
- 2 tsp. smoked Paprika
- 3/4 cup distilled white vinegar
- 1-pint glass jar; a layer of cheesecloth

Directions:

1. Combine the sugar, chilies, and salt in a bowl; Pulse the garlic until it is finely minced. Pour the mixture into a jar and push it down slightly so that the chiles are slightly buried in their liquid. Store it in a cool, dry area away from direct sunlight for at least two days and up to five days. The longer it ferments, the more active something it becomes.
2. Mix together the Paprika, achiote seeds and oil in a small saucepan over medium-high heat. Allow it to cook for 30 seconds after 2-3 minutes, or until little bubbles develop around the pan's edges. Allow to cool before straining the oil through a fine-mesh sieve into a heatproof basin.
3. Mix 2/3 of the chile combination, vinegar, and achiote oil in a blender until smooth. Fill an airtight jar halfway with the mixture.
4. Preparation is key - you can make the sauce up to 2 weeks ahead of time; just keep it cool and covered. Take notice that the spicy sauce can be made up to 1.5 times more potent than regular mayonnaise.

Per Serving:

Calories: 97| Fat: 10g| Carbs: 1g| Sodium: 543mg

Instant-pot Ancho Chile Sauce

Serving Size: 4 cups | Preparation Time: 10 mins

Ingredients:

- 2 oz. dried ancho chiles (5 to 7 chiles)
- 3 garlic cloves, lightly smashed
- 1 1/2 cups water
- 2 tsp. kosher salt
- 1 1/2 tsps. sugar
- 1/2 tsp. dried oregano
- 1/2 tsp. ground cumin
- 2 tbsps. apple cider vinegar

Directions:

1. Remove the stems and seeds from the chilies to prepare them. Put the chiles in an Instant Pot. After dealing with the chiles, properly wash your hands.
2. In an Instant Pot, combine oregano, cumin, garlic, salt, water, and sugar to pressure cook. After locking the lid, select Manual mode. Set a timer for 8 minutes and set the pressure to high. When finished, apply the natural release approach for 5 minutes, followed by the rapid release method.
3. Mix in the vinegar until smooth, and then add the remaining ingredients to make the sauce. Use it right away or store it in a sealed container in the fridge for up to a week.

Per Serving:

Calories:1224| Sodium: 305mg| Protein: 0g| Fat: 0g| Carbohydrates: 1g

☆ ☆ ☆ ☆ ☆

Green Harissa

Prep Time: 10m | Serving: 1 jar

Ingredients:

- 2 tablespoons cumin seeds
- 1 tablespoon coriander seeds
- 4 jalapeños, seeded, sliced
- 2 small scallions, sliced
- 1 small garlic clove, smashed
- 1/2 cup extra-virgin olive oil
- 1/2 cup flat-leaf parsley leaves
- 1/2 cup fresh cilantro leaves with tender stems
- 1/4 cup fresh lemon juice
- 1 teaspoon fine sea salt

Directions:

1. Toast the coriander seeds and cumin lightly in a small skillet that is set over medium heat for 2-3 minutes, stirring frequently until fragrant.
2. Puree the seeds in a food processor or blender together with the lemon juice, salt, oil, jalapenos, garlic, cilantro, parsley, and scallions until smooth.
3. Note: The harissa can be prepared 5 days in advance. Just press the surface of the harissa directly with a plastic wrap piece, and then keep it covered and chilled.

Per Serving:

Calories: 177| Carbs: 3g| Fats: 19g| Protein: 1g| Sodium: 108mg

☆ ☆ ☆ ☆ ☆

Green Goddess Sauce

Makes 7-9 Servings | Cooking + Prep Time: 20 min

Ingredients:

- 1 & 1/2 tsp. of paste, anchovy
- 1 chopped clove of garlic
- 3/4 cup of tightly packed parsley leaves
- 1/2 cup of tightly packed tarragon leaves
- 1/4 cup of tightly packed chives leaves
- 2 tbsp. of lemon juice, fresh
- 1 cup of mayonnaise, light
- 3/4 cup of yogurt, Greek
- Salt, kosher, as desired
- Pepper, ground, as desired

Directions:

1. Add garlic clove, anchovy paste, tarragon, parsley, chives leaves, and lemon juice to a food processor. Pulse several times, so the ingredients are chopped. Scrape down the food processor sides.
2. Add mayo and yogurt. Season with kosher salt and ground pepper, as desired. Blend in the food processor and stop now and then to scrape the sides down to incorporate herbs fully. The mixture is fully blended when it is bright green in color with a smooth texture. Serve promptly as a dipping sauce or over a salad.

Per Serving:

Calories: 230| Fat: 15g| Carbs: 13g| Protein: 8g| Sodium: 354mg

☆ ☆ ☆ ☆ ☆

Chimichurri Sauce

Makes 1 cup | Prep Time: 22 minutes

Ingredients:

- 1 cup of minced and packed parsley or cilantro
- 6 tbsp. of vinegar, red wine
- 2 tbsp. of oil, olive
- 2 minced garlic cloves
- 1/2 tsp. of oregano, dried
- 1/4 tsp. of salt, kosher
- 1/4 to 1/2 tsp. of crushed pepper flakes.

Directions:

1. Combine the ingredients and allow them to sit for a minimum of 15 minutes and a maximum of 2 hours at room temperature. Serve with seafood or meat.

Per Serving:

Calories: 124| Fat: 23g| Carbs: 14g| Sodium: 1034mg

☆ ☆ ☆ ☆ ☆

Enchilada Sauce

Makes 4 cups | Prep Time: 10 minutes

Ingredients:

- 28-oz. can of peeled tomatoes, whole
- 1 cup of water, filtered
- 4 tbsp. of seasoning, Southwestern or taco flavor
- 3 tbsp. of chili powder
- 1/2 chopped onion, medium
- 4 garlic cloves
- 1 de-ribbed, de-seeded jalapeno pepper
- 1/2 tsp. of kosher salt + extra if desired

Directions:

2. Blend all ingredients together in a food processor till the mixture is smooth.
3. Serve on your favorite dishes.

Per Serving:

Calories: 156| Fat: 2g| Carbs: 1.7g| Protein: 1.2g| Sodium: 1036mg

☆ ☆ ☆ ☆ ☆

Chipotle Pepper Oil

Serving: Makes about 1 cup | Preparation Time: mins

Ingredients:

- 4 dried chipotle peppers
- 1/2 cup peanut or vegetable oil

Directions:

1. Preheat the oven to 300 degrees Fahrenheit.
2. Wear rubber gloves while handling pepper seeds. Save a quarter teaspoon of the seeds.
3. Crumble the peppers into a cup metal measure or a small metal basin. Pour in the oil and save the seeds. Place a baking sheet on top of a dish or measuring cup. Cook in the lowest third of the oven for 60 minutes. Cool for 30 minutes on a rack.

Per Serving:

Calories: 84| Fat: 13g| Carbs: 5g| Sodium: 337mg

☆ ☆ ☆ ☆ ☆

Pineapple Habanero Chili Sauce

Serving: 3 cups | Preparation Time: 15 mins

Ingredients:

- 1 medium pineapple, peeled and cubed
- 1 carrot, peeled and chopped
- 1 small white onion, chopped
- 1 cup habanero pepper
- 4 garlic cloves
- 1 ½-inch ginger knob, peeled and roughly chopped
- ¼ tsp. cinnamon powder
- ½ tsp. cumin powder
- ½ tsp. turmeric powder
- ¼ cup granulated sugar
- 1 ½ cups plain vinegar
- 1 lime, zested
- Salt to taste

Directions:

1. Combine all ingredients in a food processor and blend until smooth.
2. Pour pepper sauce into sterilized jars or bottles and cover tightly.
3. Place bottles in a hot water bath for 10 minutes.
4. Remove bottles and let hot sauce age for at least 1 week before using.

Per Serving:

Calories: 234| Fat: 1g| Carbs: 12g| Sodium: 737mg

Honey-Jalapeño Sauce

Preparation Time: 10 minutes | Fermentation Duration: 10 days | Makes: 16 ounces

Ingredients:

- ¼ cup honey
- 2 garlic cloves
- ¼ cup apple cider vinegar
- 8 ounces (about 5) fresh jalapeño peppers, stemmed and halved
- 2 tablespoons non-iodized salt
- 2½ cups non-chlorinated water
- ⅛ teaspoon cumin seeds

Directions:

1. Combine the jalapenos and garlic in a clean jar. Make a brine in a separate container by mixing the water and salt.
2. If using a weight, place it on top of the jar before adding the brine, being sure to leave at least an inch of headroom.
3. The fermentation process should take around ten days, during which time the jar should be kept at ambient temperature, its cover properly screwed on, and shielded from direct sunlight. It's important to burp the jar every day.
4. After the fermentation process is finished, strain the ferment and set aside 1/4 cup of brine. In a food processor, combine the fermented vinegar, honey, the remaining brine, and cumin seeds. Blend to a smooth consistency.
5. The sauce can be kept in the refrigerator for up to a year.

Per Serving:

Calories: 260| Fat: 1g| Carbs: 2g| Sodium: 1005mg

Turmeric Jerk Sauce

Makes: 1 jar | Prep Time: 17 minutes

Ingredients:

- 60 grams of brown sugar
- 4-6 scotch bonnet peppers, seeded and cored
- 2 bunches of scallions
- 1 tsp. of turmeric
- Black pepper to taste
- 60 grams of all spice berries, ground
- 6-8 cloves of garlic
- 1 tbsp. of ground thyme
- 1 tsp. of cinnamon
- Salt to taste
- 2 tbsp. of soy sauce

Directions:

1. Add all the ingredients of the sauce to a blender.
2. Turn on the blender and blend until the contents become smooth.
3. Once the sauce is smooth, place the sauce in an airtight jar and put the jar in a refrigerator, or you could serve it immediately and enjoy.

Per Serving:

Calories: 241| Fat: 1g| Carbs: 3g| Sodium: 567mg

Smoky Chocolate-Cherry Mole

Preparation Time: 10 minutes | Fermentation Duration: 10 days | Makes: 30 ounces

Ingredients:

- ¼ cup raw pumpkin seeds
- 2½ cups non-chlorinated water
- 4 garlic cloves
- 1 dried chipotle pepper, stemmed
- 1 tablespoon white vinegar
- 1 teaspoon dried thyme
- 4 dried ancho peppers, stemmed
- 2 bay leaves
- ¼ cup cocoa powder
- 2 tablespoons non-iodized salt
- 1 onion, quartered
- 6 tablespoons granulated sugar
- 1 tablespoon honey
- 1 cup dried tart cherries
- 1 cinnamon stick
- 2 tablespoons tomato paste
- 1 teaspoon ground coriander
- 2 teaspoons cumin seeds
- 1 teaspoon dried oregano
- ¼ teaspoon salt (any kind)

Directions:

1. Mix chipotle peppers, ancho peppers, bay leaves, cherries, garlic, onion, and cinnamon stick together in a jar that has been thoroughly cleaned.
2. Create a brine by mixing the non-iodized salt with the water in a separate container.
3. After inserting a weight, if using, pour the brine into the jar, making sure to leave a headspace of at least an inch.
4. After securing the lid with a few turns of the screwdriver, place the jar somewhere out of the direct light of the sun, where it can ferment for ten days. It's important to burp the jar every day.
5. After the fermentation process is finished,

strain the ferment and set aside three-quarters of a cup of brine. The cinnamon stick should be discarded.

6. Combine the ferment, the sugar, the brine that was set aside, the cacao powder, the pumpkin seeds, the honey, the tomato paste, the cumin seeds, the vinegar, the coriander, the thyme, and the oregano in a food processor or a blender. Blend until a smooth consistency is achieved.

7. You can store the mole in the fridge for up to 6 months.

Per Serving:

Calories: 354| Fat: 14g| Carbs: 11g| Sodium: 1235mg

☆ ☆ ☆ ☆ ☆

3.2: Asia Hot Sauce Recipes

Asian Spice Hot Sauce

Prep Time: 20 mins. | Serves: 15 ounces

Ingredients:

- 3 lemon grass stalks, with the bottom section of the stalk chopped into little pieces.
- Fresh turmeric root, about 2 inches long. Peel and slice the turmeric into tiny pieces.
- 10 dried chilies
- 1-inch fermented shrimp paste.
- About 2 inches of galangal spice, peeled and then chopped fine into pieces.
- 12 candlenuts, crushed with a knife
- 3 cloves of garlic, peeled
- 20 shallots, peel the shallots and then cut into 2
- 3 tbsp. of vegetable oil

Directions:

1. Mix all of the ingredients - except for the vegetable oil - together in a blender and mix until homogeneous paste forms.
2. Heat some vegetable oil in a pan over medium heat to create a fragrant, nutty and flavorful mixture.
3. Cook the paste while swirling regularly to keep it from sticking to the pan.
4. Cook until the skillet's contents are aromatic.
5. Once the paste has gotten aromatic, remove the pan from the heat.
6. Allow the skillet to cool totally.
7. If not used right away, refrigerate the paste in sealed jars for up to one month.

Per Serving:

Calories: 30| Fat: 0g| Carbs: 1g| Sodium: 69g

☆ ☆ ☆ ☆ ☆

Vietnamese Dipping Sauce

Prep Time: 10m | Serving: 16

Ingredients:

- 2 cup fish sauce
- 1 cup rice vinegar
- 4 tbsps. water
- ¾ cup white sugar
- ¾ tsp. garlic powder
- 4 seeded and finely sliced dried red chile pepper

Directions:

1. Mix together the water, fish sauce, garlic powder, sugar, chilli pepper, and rice vinegar in a large bowl. Stir until the sugar is completely dissolved, and taste to confirm that the spicy, sweet, salty, and sour tastes are sensible. Taste again and, if necessary, adjust the spice. Fill the bottles, then cover and seal the lids.

Per Serving:

Calories: 30| Carbohydrate: 6.9 g| Total Fat: 0 g| Protein: 0.7 g| Sodium: 1094 mg

☆ ☆ ☆ ☆ ☆

Spicy Tahini Sauce

Preparation Time: 15 mins | Serving Size: 5 jars

Ingredients:

- 1 cup tahini
- 1/2 cup water
- Juice of 2 lemons
- 2 Tbsp olive oil
- 4 cloves garlic, minced
- 1/2 cup fresh cilantro, chopped
- 7 hot red chilies, seeded and chopped
- Sea salt
- 1/2 cup toasted pine nuts

Directions:

2. In a small bowl, combine lemon juice, water, and tahini until creamy and the consistency of smooth cake batter; set aside.
3. In a saucepan, heat the olive oil and sauté the garlic for 1 minute. Mix in the spicy chilies and cilantro for 1 minute. Whisk in the tahini mixture until well combined. Season with salt to taste. If necessary, add a little water to make the mixture creamy and pourable. Simmer for 5 minutes to let flavors to blend. Remove from fire, stir in toasted pine nuts, and serve hot.

Per Serving:

Calories: 225 Total Carbohydrate: 9 g Total Fat: 20 g Fiber: 3 g Protein: 6 g Sodium: 179 mg Saturated Fat: 3 g

☆ ☆ ☆ ☆ ☆

Sambal Oelek

Prep time: 10 minutes | Makes: 2 jars

Ingredients:

- 1 cup stemmed and chopped red jalapeños
- 6 fresh Thai chiles, stemmed and chopped
- 1 teaspoon salt
- 1 teaspoon granulated sugar
- 4 teaspoons freshly squeezed lime juice

Directions:

1. Mix together the jalapenos, chiles, salt, sugar, and lime juice in a blender or food processor to create a paste that is just beginning to thicken.
2. Keep refrigerated for up to a week.

Per Serving:

Calories: 32| Fat: 0 g| Carbs: 11g| Sodium: 189mg

☆ ☆ ☆ ☆ ☆

Sticky Sweet Chili Sauce

Prep time: 15 minutes | Cook time: 3 minutes | Makes 20 ounces

Ingredients:

- 1-ounce dried Thai chiles, stemmed (about 30 peppers)
- 8 garlic cloves
- ¾ cup cane sugar
- ⅔ cup water
- ½ cup unseasoned rice vinegar
- 1 tablespoon tapioca starch
- 2 teaspoons salt

Directions:

1. Cover the dried chiles with boiling water and put aside for 10 minutes or until tender.
2. Place the softened chilies in a blender or food processor. In a mixing bowl, whisk together the garlic, sugar, water, vinegar, tapioca starch, and salt. Blend until almost entirely smooth.
3. In a small saucepan, bring the sauce to a boil over high heat. Boil for 3 minutes, then remove from the heat. Allow the sauce to come to room temperature. The sauce will thicken even more as it cools.
4. Refrigerate for up to a month.

Per Serving:

Calories: 45| Fat: 1g| Carbs: 1g| Sodium: 602mg

☆ ☆ ☆ ☆ ☆

Nuoc Cham

Prep time: 10 minutes | Makes 15 ounces

Ingredients:

- ¾ cup water
- ¼ cup freshly squeezed lime juice
- 3 tablespoons granulated sugar
- 3 tablespoons fish sauce
- 4 fresh Thai chiles, stemmed and sliced paper-thin
- 1 garlic clove, finely chopped

Directions:

1. In a jar with a tight-fitting cover, combine the water, lime juice, and sugar. Shake the jar vigorously to dissolve the sugar.
2. In a mixing bowl, combine the fish sauce, chilies, and garlic. Stir everything together to blend.
3. Refrigerate for up to two weeks.

Per Serving:

Calories: 60 | Cars: 5g | Protein: 1g Fat: 1g Sodium: 1204mg Potassium: 54mg Fiber: 1g Vitamin C: 5mg Calcium: 6mg

☆ ☆ ☆ ☆ ☆

Fermented Thai-Style Green Curry Sauce

Prep time: 20 minutes | Fermentation time: 10 days | Makes 40 ounces

Ingredients:

- 6 fresh Thai green chiles or serrano peppers, stemmed and halved lengthwise 1 shallot, halved
- 6 scallions, green and white parts, halved
- 3 stalks of fresh lemongrass, halved
- 1-inch knob of fresh ginger root, peeled
- 5 garlic cloves, peeled
- 2½ cups non-chlorinated water
- 2 tablespoons non-iodized salt
- 1 (12-ounce) can of coconut milk
- 1 teaspoon cumin seeds
- ¼ cup fresh chopped cilantro
- ¼ cup lime juice
- 1 tablespoon granulated sugar
- 1 teaspoon salt
- 1 teaspoon ground turmeric
- ½ teaspoon ground coriander
- ½ teaspoon freshly ground black pepper

Directions:

1. In a clean jar, combine the chilies, shallot, scallions, lemongrass, ginger, and garlic.
2. Store in an airtight container away from direct sunshine for 2 weeks, burping it every day to keep it cool and free from micro-fungal irritations.
3. After fermentation is complete, strain the ferment and save 14 cups of the brine.
4. In a food processor or blender, combine the fermented coconut milk, saved brine, cumin seeds, cilantro, lime juice, sugar, salt, turmeric, coriander, and black pepper. Blend on high until totally smooth.
5. Refrigerate for up to three weeks.

Per Serving:

Calories: 18| Fat: 1g| Carbs: 1g| Sodium: 362mg

Smooth Serrano-Cilantro Mint Chutney

Prep time: 14 minutes | Makes 25 ounces

Ingredients:

- 2 cups fresh chopped cilantro
- 2 cups fresh mint leaves
- 5 serrano peppers, stemmed and chopped
- ½ cup chopped red onion
- 4 tablespoons lemon juice
- ½ teaspoon salt

Directions:

1. In a blender or food processor, combine the cilantro, mint, pepper, onion, lemon juice, and salt. Blend until smooth paste forms.
2. Refrigerate for up to a week.

Per Serving:

Calories: 60| Fat: 1g| Carbs: 1g| Sodium: 462mg

☆ ☆ ☆ ☆ ☆

Lemon Achar

Preparation Time: 15 mins | Serving Size: 1 jar

Ingredients:

- 12 red Thai chiles, thinly sliced*
- 4 Meyer lemons, quartered, seeded, and thinly sliced
- 5 cloves garlic, thinly sliced
- 1 (1-inch) piece of ginger, thinly sliced
- 1½ tablespoons grated fresh turmeric
- 1 teaspoon toasted brown mustard seeds
- ½ teaspoon toasted cumin seeds
- ½ teaspoon toasted fenugreek seeds
- 1 teaspoon salt
- Juice of 1 lemon
- 4 tablespoons olive oil

Directions:

1. In a large mixing bowl, combine the chiles, lemons, garlic, ginger, and turmeric. Toss in the toasted spices, including mustard seeds, cumin seeds, and fenugreek seeds. Mix in the salt, lemon juice, and 2 tablespoons of olive oil.
2. Fill a jar just big enough for your ferment with the ingredients. Pour the remaining 2 tablespoons of olive oil over the top of the mixture and tighten the jar cover.
3. Place the jar in a bright location for 7 to 14 days to ferment. When it's done, it'll taste pickle-y sour.
4. This ferment may be stored in the refrigerator for up to 12 months.

Per Serving:

Calories: 56| Fat: 15g| Carbs: 11g| Sodium: 162mg

☆ ☆ ☆ ☆ ☆

Rhubarb Achar

Prep Time: 15 mins | Serving Size: 6 cups

Ingredients:

- 1-pound rhubarb (2–3 medium stalks), sliced microthin crosswise at an angle
- 4 cloves garlic, sliced thinly
- 1 tablespoon grated fresh turmeric
- ½ teaspoon salt
- 3 tablespoons Basic Go-To Mash
- 1 teaspoon black mustard seeds, toasted and ground
- 1 teaspoon Szechuan pepper, toasted and ground
- ½ teaspoon fennel seeds, toasted and ground
- ½ teaspoon fenugreek seeds, toasted and ground

Directions:

1. Mix together the rhubarb, garlic, turmeric, and pepper in a bowl with some salt and massage it in. Mix in the mustard seeds, Szechuan pepper, fennel seeds, and fenugreek seeds. At this point, the mixture should be moist with a chutney-like consistency.
2. Fill a jar halfway with the mixture, pushing out any air pockets as you go. Place a zipper bag over the surface of the ferment, fill it with water, and zip it shut.
3. Place the jar in a kitchen corner to ferment. Remove the bag, push the ferment down with a clean utensil, rinse the bag, and replace it if you find air pockets.
4. Allow it to ferment longer for extra sourness and punch. This ferment's hues will fade, and the brine will turn hazy as it finishes fermenting.
5. Place the ferment in the refrigerator and cover it with a lid to keep it fresh for up to 6 months.

Per Serving:

Calories: 77| Fat: 1g| Carbs: 1g| Sodium: 345mg

☆ ☆ ☆ ☆ ☆

Satay Sauce

Makes: 2 cups | Prep Time: 15 minutes

Ingredients:

- 1 cup of unsalted peanuts, dry roasted
- 1/3 cup of water, filtered
- 1-2 minced garlic cloves
- 1/2 tsp. of soy sauce, dark
- 2 tsp. of oil, sesame
- 2 tbsp. of sugar, brown
- 1 & 1/2 tbsp. of soy sauce, light
- 1/2 tbsp. of lime juice, fresh if available
- 1 tsp. of pepper, cayenne, +/- as desired
- 1/3 cup of milk, coconut

Directions:

1. Place ingredients in a food processor or blender.
2. Process or blend till the sauce has a smooth texture. Taste and adjust if desired. Serve while it is still warm as a topping for beef, pork, chicken satay, or with any favorite dish it will complement.

Per Serving:

Calories: 209| Fat: 13g| Carbs: 12.7g| Protein: 2.2g| Sodium: 236mg

Indian-Style Chutney Sauce

Makes: 4-6 Servings | Prep Time: 20 minutes

Ingredients:

- 1/2 of a medium grated coconut, fresh
- 2 tbsp. of oil, vegetable
- 1 tsp. of mustard seeds, black
- 5-6 finely chopped curry leaves
- 5 finely chopped red chilies, dry
- 1 tbsp. of roasted chickpeas or yellow lentils
- Kosher salt, as desired

Directions:

1. Grind coconut into a fine paste with a food processor. Reserve.
2. Heat oil in a small-sized pan. When the oil has heated, add curry leaves, mustard seeds, lentils (or chickpeas), and chilies.
3. Stir frequently while sautéing the mixture, so it won't burn. When done, it will be aromatic and a bit darker in color.
4. Remove pan from heat. Add to coconut paste made in step 1 above. Combine well and add kosher salt, as desired. Serve on or with your favorite Indian dish.

Per Serving:

Calories: 234| Fat: 1g| Carbs: 1g| Sodium: 678mg

☆ ☆ ☆ ☆ ☆

Momos Chutney

Preparation Time: 10 minutes | Fermentation Duration: 10 days | Makes: 18 ounces

Ingredients:

- 1 teaspoon granulated sugar
- 1 teaspoon Szechuan peppercorns
- 3 medium Roma tomatoes, halved
- 4 garlic cloves
- 1 ounce (about 5) dried Kashmiri or ancho peppers, stemmed
- 2½ cups non-chlorinated water
- ¼ teaspoon black peppercorns
- 2 tablespoons non-iodized salt

Directions:

1. Mix the tomatoes, garlic, chilies, and peppercorns together in a jar that has been thoroughly cleaned. To prepare the brine, combine the water and salt in a separate container and stir until the salt is dissolved.
2. After inserting a weight, if using, pour the brine into the jar, making sure to leave a headspace of at least an inch.
3. Put the lid on tightly and leave the jar at room temperature and out of direct sunlight for 10 days to ferment. It's important to burp the jar every day.
4. After the fermentation process is finished, strain the ferment and set aside a half cup of brine.
5. Combine the ferment, the brine that was reserved, and the sugar in a food processor or blender. Blend until a smooth consistency is achieved.
6. The sauce can be kept in the fridge for up to a year.

Per Serving:

Calories: 254| Fat: 0g| Carbs: 1.7g| Sodium: 876mg

☆ ☆ ☆ ☆ ☆

La Jiao Jiang (Hot Chili Sauce)

Preparation Time: 10 minutes | Fermentation Duration: 7 days | Makes: 15 ounces

Ingredients:

- 2 tablespoons non-iodized salt
- 4 medium red bell peppers, sliced into strips
- 1½ ounces (about 36) fresh Thai peppers, stemmed
- 2½ cups non-chlorinated water
- 1 garlic clove
- ¼ cup rice vinegar

Directions:

1. Combine the bell peppers, Thai peppers, and garlic in a jar that has been thoroughly cleaned. To prepare the brine, combine the water and salt in a separate container and stir until the salt is dissolved.
2. After inserting a weight, if using, pour the brine into the jar, making sure to leave a headspace of at least an inch.
3. After firmly screwing on the lid, place the jar somewhere out of the direct light of the sun, where it can ferment for a week at room temperature. It's important to burp the jar every day.
4. After the fermentation process is finished, strain the ferment and set aside a quarter cup of brine.
5. Blend or process the ferment, the vinegar, and the brine that was reserved together in a food processor or blender. Blend until a smooth consistency is achieved.
6. The sauce can be kept in the fridge for up to a year.

Per Serving:

Calories: 231| Fat: 0g| Carbs: 1.7g| Sodium: 1043mg

☆ ☆ ☆ ☆ ☆

Hot and orange dressing

Preparation Time: Depends | Servings: 4-6

Ingredients:

- ½ cup yellow bell peppers, diced
- 1 tbsp. minced garlic
- 1 tbsp. honey
- 1 tsp. sea salt
- 2/3 cup white balsamic vinegar
- 2 tbsp. water

Directions:

1. First, in a medium saucepan, place all the ingredients and bring the heat to medium-high.
2. Stir often and turn down the heat once it is bubbling.
3. Let it cook for another 15 minutes.
4. Next, remove it from the heat and let it cool down.
5. Place the mixture in the blender and activate until the mixture becomes smooth, consistence with a sauce.
6. Refrigerate in a container of your choice until ready to eat.

Per Serving:

Calories: 100| Fat: 1g| Carbs: 1.7g| Sodium: 1098mg

She Simmers Sauce

Serving Size: 2 cups | Preparation Time: 5 mins

Ingredients:

- 8 fresh red, yellow, or orange habanero chiles
- ½ cup freshly squeezed orange juice
- ½ cup distilled white vinegar
- 2 tablespoons freshly squeezed lemon juice
- 2 tablespoons freshly squeezed lime juice
- 1 teaspoon salt
- 2 teaspoons freshly ground black pepper
- 4 garlic cloves, minced
- 2 tablespoons minced fresh ginger
- 1 tablespoon curry powder
- 1 teaspoon ground allspice
- ½ teaspoon ground or freshly grated nutmeg
- ½ teaspoon ground cinnamon

Directions:

1. Reserve the seeds after stemming and seeding the habaneros. Blend the chiles with the remaining ingredients in a blender until smooth. Add a dusting of the seeds if you want to increase the heat.
2. Fill bottles with the mixture and refrigerate.

Per Serving:

Calories: 45| Fat: 5g| Carbs: 7g| Sodium: 487mg

☆ ☆ ☆ ☆ ☆

Cantaloupe Chutney

Preparation Time: 1hr 3omin | Servings: 4 pints

Ingredients:

- 3 medium cantaloupes
- 1 pound of dried apricots
- 1 fresh hot chili
- 2 cups of raisins
- 1 tsp. ground cloves
- 1 tsp. ground nutmeg
- 2 tbsps. salt
- 2 tbsps. mustard seed
- 1/4 cup fresh ginger, chopped
- 3 cloves garlic
- 4-1/2 cups apple cider vinegar
- 2-1/4 cups brown sugar
- 4 onions
- 1/2 cup orange juice
- 2 tbsps. orange zest
- cinnamon

Directions:

1. Thinly slice the apricots and put them into a large bowl. Chop the ginger and garlic thinly and add to the dish. Stir in chili, seed, and dice, and add to the pot.
2. Add raisins, cloves, cinnamon, nutmeg, and mustard seeds. Mix together and set aside. Mix the vinegar and sugar in a non-reactive pot or kettle; bring to a boil over medium heat.
3. Add mixture to the pot in a bowl and return to a moderate simmer. Keep simmer for 45 minutes. Do not deck the pot.
4. Meanwhile, chop the onions and place them in a bowl. Peel and seed the Cantaloupes. Split the fruit into cubes of ½ inches. Add onions. In a cup, add orange juice and zest; mix well.
5. Once the vinegar mixture has been cooked for 45 minutes, add the cantaloupe mixture to the bowl, bring it back to a cooler, and start cooking for another 45 minutes or until thickened at the simmer.
6. Pour into hot glasses, making sure to clean the rims of each glass. Screw the lid and ring onto each glass to keep them in place. Boiling water bath process: pints and quarts 10 minutes in both.

Per Serving:

Calories: 54| Fat: 1g| Carbs: 1.7g| Sodium: 100mg

☆ ☆ ☆ ☆ ☆

Flavorful Teriyaki Jerky

Preparation Time: 15 mins | Servings: 6

Ingredients:

- 1 ½ lbs. beef bottom round thin meat
- 1 tsp onion powder
- 1 tsp garlic, minced
- 1 tsp red pepper flakes
- 1/3 cup soy sauce
- 1/3 cup Worcestershire sauce
- 1 tsp liquid smoke
- ½ cup teriyaki sauce

Directions:

1. Cut meat into thin slices.
2. Add teriyaki sauce, onion powder, garlic, red pepper flakes, soy sauce, Worcestershire sauce, and liquid smoke in the large bowl.
3. Add meat slices to the bowl and mix until well coated. Cover bowl tightly and place in refrigerator overnight.
4. Place marinated meat slices on dehydrator trays and dehydrate at 160 F/ 71 C for 5-6 hours.
5. Store in an air-tight container.

Per Serving:

Calories: 246| Fat: 1g| Carbs: 1.7g| Sodium: 1098mg

☆ ☆ ☆ ☆ ☆

Jalapeño syrup

Serving Size: 1 cup | Preparation Time: 3 mins

Ingredients:

- 1 sliced jalapeño pepper
- 8 tablespoons water
- 1 cup demerara sugar

Directions:

1. Boil the sugar in a pan of water.
2. Stir till the sugar is melted.
3. Throw in the jalapeño.
4. Cook for 4 minutes.
5. Set aside to cool and steep before straining into a container.
6. Serve or store.

Per Serving:

Calories: 45| Fat: 0g| Carbs: 0g| Sodium: 45mg

Beef Skirt with Chili Sauce

Total Prep Time: 20 minutes | Yield: 2 to 3 servings

Ingredients:

- Arepas – 4, cooked
- Beef skirt – 2 pounds
- Onion – ½ cup, chopped
- Garlic cloves2, minced
- Red chilies chopped – 1 cup
- Red chili sauce – 2 tablespoons
- Scallions – 2, chopped
- Ground cumin – 1 teaspoon
- Beer – ½ cup
- Oil – 4 tablespoons
- Salt and pepper to taste
- Cilantro – ½ cup

Directions:

1. Add oil to a pan.
2. Mix onion, garlic cloves, scallions, and cumin with salt and pepper in a bowl.
3. Dip the beef skirt in the mixture. Add red chili and red chili sauce.
4. Place into the pan. Cook for 20 minutes on both sides.
5. When ready, place it on the arepa.
6. Garnish cilantro to serve!

Nutrition:

Calories: 50 calories; Carbs: 5.9 Protein: 2.7 Fat: 5.3

☆ ☆ ☆ ☆ ☆

Crabby Dish

Total Prep Time: 25 minutes | Yield: 2 to 3 servings

Ingredients:

- Oil – 2 tablespoons
- Crabs swimmers – 1 lb.
- Garlic cloves crushed – 2
- Red long chilies – 2 chopped
- Fresh chopped ginger – 2 tablespoons
- Chili sauce – 2 tablespoons
- Brown sugar – 2 tablespoons
- Coriander chopped – 2 cups

Directions:

1. Heat the pan with oil.
2. Add garlic and crab. Cook for 2 minutes.
3. Keep stirring, and then add ginger, chili sauce, brown sugar and long red chilies.
4. Cook for 20 minutes.
5. When done, dress with coriander to serve!

Nutrition:

Calories: 50 calories; Carbs: 5.9 Protein: 2.7 Fat: 5.3

☆ ☆ ☆ ☆ ☆

Hot Red Beans

Total Prep Time: 15 minutes | Yield: 3 to 4 servings

Ingredients:

- Red chilies chopped – 1 cup
- Red chili sauce – 2 tablespoons
- Eggs 2
- Red beans (boiled) – 2 cups
- Green pepper 1/2 cup
- Tomato chopped 2
- Salt and pepper to taste

Directions:

1. Chop green pepper and tomatoes well and mix them together in a bowl.
2. Add salt and pepper to it as needed. Now beat the eggs in it and mix well. Stir it all together really well to make a thick texture.
3. Cook for 20 minutes, and then add red beans, red chili and sauce. Stir well.
4. When ready, serve!

Nutrition:

Calories: 40 calories; Carbs: 5.5; Protein: 2.7 Fat: 6.3

☆ ☆ ☆ ☆ ☆

Chili Sauce and Tomatoes

Total Prep Time: 30 minutes | Yield: 4 to 5 servings

Ingredients:

- Chicken boneless – 3 pieces
- Potatoes 4
- Tomatoes 4
- Water – 2 cups
- Red chilies chopped – 1 cup
- Red chili sauce – 2 tablespoons
- Tomato paste 1 can
- Salt and pepper to taste
- Basil 1/2 chopped
- Oil 2 tablespoons

Directions:

1. Wash the chicken well and then put hot water in the pot. When it boils, add the chicken in it and let it boil for about 15 minutes.
2. Meanwhile, cut the potatoes and keep them as a base in the baking dish. Turn on the heat of the oven to 400 F.
3. Now bake the potatoes for 10 minutes while the chicken boils.
4. Meanwhile, combine the tomato sauce and oil. Mix it thoroughly with the tomatoes, then add the red chili and red chili sauce to make it thick. Now add salt and pepper as needed.
5. When everything is cooked, take a plate and put the chicken as a base, followed by the potato slices and then pour the tomato sauce on it with a sprinkling of the chopped basil on it, and it is ready to eat now!

Nutrition:

Calories: 50 calories; Carbs: 5.9 Protein: 2.7 Fat: 5.3

☆ ☆ ☆ ☆ ☆

Hot Shrimp Dish

Total Prep Time: 25 minutes | Yield: 2 to 3 servings

Ingredients:

- Fried green plantains – 2
- Guacamole – 1 cup
- Shrimps – 1 lb.
- Oil – 2 tablespoons
- Red chilies chopped – 1 cup
- Red chili sauce – 2 tablespoons
- Garlic cloves – 2 minced
- Paprika – 1 teaspoon
- Ground cumin – 1 tablespoon
- Lime for serving
- Salt and pepper to taste

Directions:

1. Add oil to a pot on low heat.
2. Mix shrimps, guacamole and green plantain. Cook for 15 minutes.
3. Add garlic cloves, paprika, and ground cumin with salt and pepper. Add red chili and red chili sauce.
4. Cook for another 10 minutes.
5. When ready, garnish lime to serve!

Nutrition:

Calories: 50 calories; Carbs: 5.9 Protein: 2.7 Fat: 5.3

☆ ☆ ☆ ☆ ☆

Hot Eggplant

Total Prep Time: 20 minutes | Yield: 3 to 4 servings

Ingredients:

- Potatoes 2
- Onion chopped – 2
- Red Pepper – 1 tablespoon
- Red chilies chopped – 1 cup
- Red chili sauce – 2 tablespoons
- Garlic cloves 2
- Tomato – 2
- Oil – 2 tablespoons
- Salt and pepper to taste
- Water hot, ½ cup

Directions:

1. Add oil to a pan. Cut the vegetables in the same shape and equal sizes. Add onion, potatoes, eggplant, and red pepper to the pan.
2. Mix them all well and sprinkle salt on them as needed. Now mince the garlic clove and sprinkle them over the mixture.
3. Now as it cooks, by the end, add the tomatoes with red chili and red chili sauce on the top and cover the pan. Check after 5 minutes and add half a cup of water to it.
4. Cover it again and let it cook on low flame for about 15 minutes. When done, serve it with rice or pita bread.

Nutrition:

Calories: 50 calories; Carbs: 5.9 Protein: 2.7 Fat: 5.3

☆ ☆ ☆ ☆ ☆

Cauliflower with Cheese Sauce

Total Prep Time: 25 minutes | Yield: 2 to 3 servings

Ingredients:

- Cauliflower 1 – florets separate
- Red chilies chopped – 1 cup
- Red chili sauce – 2 tablespoons
- Vinegar 1/2 tablespoons
- Salt to taste
- For Sauce
- Milk 1/2 cup
- Basil – a bunch of chopped

Directions:

1. Cut the cauliflower and wash it gently with cold water. Now turn on the oven to 350 F and place the cauliflowers in the baking dish.
2. Add red chili and red chili sauce. Mix well.
3. Cook them half way and then add the sauce.
4. Take a bowl and add milk and basil to it. Mix it well, cover the baking dish with this sauce and sprinkle cheese over it.
5. Let it bake for about 20 minutes, and when ready, serve immediately.

Nutrition:

Calories: 50 calories; Carbs: 5.9 Protein: 2.7 Fat: 5.3

☆ ☆ ☆ ☆ ☆

Chipotle Pepper Oil

Serving: 1 jar | Cooking Time: 30 minutes

Ingredients:

- 2 dried chipotle peppers*
- 1/2 cup peanut or vegetable oil

Directions:

1. Start preheating the oven to 300°F.
2. Take peppers seeds while wearing rubber gloves. Save a quarter teaspoon of seeds.
3. Crumble the peppers into a 1-cup metal measure or a small metal bowl. Pour in the oil and reserved seeds. Place a baking sheet on top of a bowl or measuring cup. Cook in the lower third of the oven for 60 minutes. Cool for 30 minutes on a rack.
4. Line several cheesecloth layers on a small strainer. Strain the oil into the glass jar. Cover the flavored oil loosely and keep it in the refrigerator at all times for up to one month.

Per Serving:

Calories: 1024| Fat: 3g| Carbs: 26g| Protein: 3g

☆ ☆ ☆ ☆ ☆

Hot Potato Mix

Total Prep Time: 35 minutes | Yield: 2 to 3 servings

Ingredients:

- Cauliflower cut – 1
- Potatoes peeled and chunks – 3
- Oil – 1 tablespoon
- Cumin seeds – 1 tablespoon
- Red chilies chopped – 1 cup
- Red chili sauce – 2 tablespoons
- Tomatoes diced – 2
- Salt to taste
- Curry powder – 1 teaspoon

Directions:

1. Cook the cauliflower florets in the microwave for about 4 minutes. When they are soft and tender, take the bowl outside and set it aside.
2. Take a dish, place the potatoes in it, and microwave for 5 minutes. When done, mix them with the cauliflower.
3. Get a skillet and heat oil in it by mixing cumin seeds in it. After it is cooked, add onions and tomatoes to cook for about 5 minutes. Now add red chilies and red chili sauce.
4. When cooked, add cauliflower and potatoes in it and season it with curry powder and salt according to your taste.

Nutrition:

Calories: 50 calories; Carbs: 5.9 Protein: 2.7 Fat: 5.3

☆ ☆ ☆ ☆ ☆

AMBA

Preparation Time: 10 minutes | Fermentation Duration: 5 days | Makes: 16 ounces

Ingredients:

- 1 teaspoon cumin seeds
- 2 tablespoons non-iodized salt
- 1/10 ounce (about 4) dried cayenne peppers, stemmed
- 2 mangos, peeled and diced
- 1 teaspoon fenugreek
- 2½ cups non-chlorinated water
- 1 teaspoon mustard seeds
- 1 garlic clove
- 1 tablespoon granulated sugar
- ¼ cup lemon juice

Directions:

1. Mix the garlic, chilies, and mangoes in a jar that has been thoroughly cleaned. To prepare the brine, combine the water and salt in a separate container and stir until the salt is dissolved.
2. After placing a weight on top of the jar, if you are using one, pour the brine inside while leaving at least an inch of headspace.
3. After firmly screwing on the lid, place the jar somewhere out of the direct sunshine where it can ferment for five days at room temperature. It's important to burp the jar every day.
4. After the fermentation process is finished, strain the ferment and set aside 1/4 cup of brine.
5. Combine the ferment, the cumin seeds, the brine that was reserved, the fenugreek seeds, the lemon juice, the mustard seeds, and the sugar in a food processor or blender. Blend until a smooth consistency is achieved.
6. You can preserve the sauce in the refrigerator for up to six months without spoiling.

Banana Ketchup

Preparation Time: 10 minutes | Fermentation Duration: 7 days | Makes: 20 ounces

Ingredients:

- ¼ cup tomato paste
- 1 white or yellow onion, halved
- ½ cup white vinegar
- 1½ ounces (about 5) fresh jalapeño peppers
- 2 garlic cloves
- 1 (2-inch) piece of fresh ginger
- 2 tablespoons non-iodized salt
- ¼ cup granulated sugar
- 2½ cups non-chlorinated water
- 2 bananas, peeled
- ¼ teaspoon salt (any kind)

Directions:

1. Mix the jalapeños, ginger, onion, and garlic in a jar that has been thoroughly cleaned. Create a brine by mixing the non-iodized salt with the water in a separate container.
2. After placing a weight on top of the jar, if you are using one, pour the brine inside while leaving at least an inch of headspace.
3. After firmly screwing on the lid, place the jar somewhere out of the direct light of the sun, where it can ferment for one week at room temperature. It's important to burp the jar every day.
4. After the fermentation process is finished, strain the ferment and set aside a quarter cup of brine.
5. Combine the ferment, the vinegar, the bananas, the brine that you conserved, the salt, the sugar, and the tomato paste in a blender or food processor. Blend until the mixture is completely smooth.
6. The sauce can be kept in the fridge for up to 9 months.

Per Serving:

Calories: 342| Fat: 5g| Carbs: 15g| Sodium: 867mg

☆ ☆ ☆ ☆ ☆

Per Serving:

Calories: 109| Fat: 1g| Carbs: 10g| Sodium: 1035mg

☆ ☆ ☆ ☆ ☆

ZHUG

Preparation Time: 10 minutes | Fermentation Duration: 5 days | Makes: 16 ounces

Ingredients:

- 1 teaspoon cumin seeds
- 6 garlic cloves
- ¾ cup packed fresh cilantro
- 1 cup packed fresh parsley
- 3 green cardamom pods
- ½ cup olive oil for serving
- 1/10 ounce (about 5) dried chiles de Arbol, stemmed
- 3 ounces (about 7) fresh serrano peppers, stemmed
- ½ teaspoon black peppercorns
- 1 teaspoon coriander seeds
- 2½ cups non-chlorinated water
- ½ cup lemon juice
- 2 tablespoons non-iodized salt

Directions:

1. Combine the parsley, serrano peppers, cilantro, Chile de Arbol, cardamom pods, black peppercorns, cumin seeds, garlic, and coriander seeds in a clean container.
2. Make a brine in a separate container by mixing the water and salt. After placing a weight on top of the jar, if you are using one, pour the brine inside while leaving at least an inch of headspace.
3. The jar should be kept at room temperature and out of direct sunlight for 5 days to ferment. It's important to burp the jar every day.
4. After the fermentation process is finished, strain the ferment and set aside 1/4 cup of brine. Combine the ferment, the reserved brine, and the lemon juice in a food processor or a blender. Blend until smooth.
5. You can preserve the sauce in the refrigerator for up to three months. Before serving, combine 1 tbsp of olive oil with 1/4 cup of sauce.

Iran Pepper Hot Sauce

Preparation Time: 10 minutes | Makes: 1 Jar

Ingredients:

- 4 cloves of garlic, grated
- 1 lime
- 1 tsp. of cumin, ground
- ½ tsp. of pepper
- 3 bunches of fresh saffron, washed and dried
- 8 small Iran red peppers, remove the stems
- 1 tsp. of cardamom, ground
- 1 tsp. of salt
- 120 ml of olive oil

Directions:

1. Add the saffron to the bowl of a food processor.
2. Turn on the processor and process at low speed to shred the saffron.
3. Next, add the juice of one lime. Also, add some olive oil.
4. Now, pulse the contents of the food processor to form a paste.
5. Next, add the garlic. Pulse the contents of the food processor to mix and combine well.
6. Now, add the red chilies to the contents of the bowl.
7. Again, pulse the contents of the bowl until well incorporated.
8. Now, add the cardamom. Also, add some salt to season.
9. Now, add the pepper. Next, add the cumin.
10. Process the contents of the food processor until smooth and well mixed and combined.
11. You can then place the zhug in an airtight container and put the container in the refrigerator for up to 3 weeks.
12. You could also place the container in the freezer for up to 6 months.

Per Serving:

Calories: 181| Fat: 15g| Carbs: 11.7g| Sodium: 235mg

☆ ☆ ☆ ☆ ☆

Per Serving:

Calories: 100| Fat: 1g| Carbs: 1.7g| Sodium: 1098mg

☆ ☆ ☆ ☆ ☆

Spicy Coconut-Mint Chutney

Preparation Time: 10 minutes | Fermentation Duration: 5 days | Makes: 12 ounces

Ingredients:

- 1 tablespoon mustard seeds
- 2 tablespoons non-iodized salt
- 1 ounce (about 4) fresh serrano peppers, stemmed
- 2 cups packed fresh mint leaves
- 2½ cups non-chlorinated water
- 1 (½-inch) piece of fresh ginger
- ¼ cup shredded unsweetened coconut
- 3 tablespoons tamarind paste

Directions:

1. Mix the ginger, chilies, and mint together in a container that has been thoroughly cleaned. To prepare the brine, combine the water and salt in a separate container and stir until the salt is dissolved.
2. After inserting a weight, if using, pour the brine into the jar, making sure to leave a headspace of at least an inch.
3. After firmly screwing on the lid, place the jar somewhere out of the direct sunshine where it can ferment for five days at room temperature. It's important to burp the jar every day.
4. After the fermentation process is finished, strain the ferment and set aside a half cup of brine.
5. Mix the ferment, the coconut, the reserved brine, the mustard seeds, and the tamarind in a food processor or a blender. Blend until a smooth consistency is achieved.
6. The sauce can be kept in the fridge for up to three months.

Per Serving:

Calories: 250| Fat: 1g| Carbs: 27g| Sodium: 1145mg

☆ ☆ ☆ ☆ ☆

3.3: Europe Hot Sauce Recipes

Kale Pesto Sauce

Makes: 1 cup | Prep Time: 10 minutes

Ingredients:

- 2 cups of kale, torn, without stems
- Parsley, fresh, as desired to mix with the kale
- 1/2 cup of oil, olive
- 1/4 tsp. of salt, kosher + extra if desired
- 1 garlic clove
- 1 fresh lemon, juice only
- 1/4 – 1/2 cup of almonds, raw
- 1 tsp. of pepper, cayenne, +/- as desired

Directions:

1. Combine the kale and parsley.
2. Pulse the kale mixture with oil, kosher salt, Cayenne, lemon juice, and garlic in a food processor till you have a smooth texture.
3. Add almonds. Pulse till they are ground to the desired consistency.
4. Serve with pasta, pizza, crackers, salads, eggs, sandwiches, soup, or your favorite dish.

Per Serving:

Calories: 181| Fat: 15g| Carbs: 11.7g| Sodium: 235mg

☆ ☆ ☆ ☆ ☆

Beurre Blanc Sauce

Makes: 12 Servings | Prep Time: 40 minutes

Ingredients:

- 1 & 1/2 tbsp. of shallot, chopped
- 8 peppercorns
- 1 bay leaf
- 1/4 cup of vinegar, white wine
- 2 tbsp. of dry wine, white
- 1/4 cup of cream, heavy
- 1 & 1/2 cups of cubed, cold butter, unsalted

Directions:

1. Place the shallot, peppercorns, bay leaf, wine, and vinegar in a medium pan. Bring mixture to boil. Reduce the heat level to med. Continue to simmer till there is only 2 tbsp. liquid in the pan.
2. Add heavy cream. Bring to a simmer. Continue simmering till the cream has been reduced by 1/2. Raise heat level to med-high. Whisk in butter rapidly, cube by cube, till it melts into the cream and thickens it.
3. Remove spices by straining the sauce through a mesh strainer. Serve with fish or your favorite side dish.

Per Serving:

Calories: 260| Fat: 1g| Carbs: 27g| Sodium: 345mg

☆ ☆ ☆ ☆ ☆

Romesco Sauce

Makes: 4 Servings | Prep Time: 10 minutes

Ingredients:

- 12-oz. jar of drained red peppers, roasted
- 4 plum tomatoes, small
- 1 cup of almonds, raw
- 1/4 cup of parsley, fresh
- 1/4 cup of oil, olive
- 1 tsp. of salt, kosher + more if desired
- 2 garlic cloves
- 1/2 fresh lemon, juice only

Directions:

1. Pulse all ingredients together in a food processor till you like their texture.
2. Serve cold or hot on your favorite dish.

Per Serving:

Calories: 235| Fat: 2g| Carbs: 1g| Sodium: 645mg

☆ ☆ ☆ ☆ ☆

Hollandaise Sauce

Makes: 8 Servings | Prep Time: 35 minutes

Ingredients:

- 1 cup of butter, clarified
- 4 egg yolks, large
- 1 tbsp. of water, cold
- 2 tbsp. of lemon juice, freshly squeezed
- Kosher salt, as desired
- Cayenne pepper, as desired

Directions:

1. Heat 1-2" of filtered water in a pan on med. heat. Butter should be warmed, yet not hot.
2. Combine cold water and egg yolks in a steel or glass mixing bowl. Whisk for a couple of minutes till the mixture is foamy and light. Whisk in 2-3 drops of lemon juice.
3. Once the water in the pan is simmering, set the bowl on top of the pan, ensuring that water does not touch the bowl's bottom. Whisk egg mixture till thickened slightly, 1-2 minutes.
4. Remove bowl from heat. Whisk constantly as you slowly add clarified butter, several drops at a time.
5. Continue to beat clarified butter. You can add it a bit faster as your sauce thickens.
6. After all the butter has been added, whisk in the remainder of lemon juice. Season with kosher salt, and cayenne pepper, as desired.
7. Hollandaise sauce, when finished, should have a firm, smooth consistency. If it seems too thick, whisk in several drops of lukewarm water. Serve.

Per Serving:

Calories: 234| Fat: 34g| Carbs: 23g| Sodium: 1034mg

☆ ☆ ☆ ☆ ☆

Easy Marinara Sauce

Makes: 2 cups | Prep Time: 55 minutes

Ingredients:

- 1 x 28-oz. can of tomatoes, whole, peeled
- 1 peeled, halved medium onion, yellow
- 2 large, peeled whole garlic cloves
- 2 tbsp. of oil, olive
- 1 tsp. of oregano, dried
- ½ tbs pepper flakes, red
- Kosher salt, as desired

Directions:

1. In a medium pan, combine tomatoes and their juice, onion, cloves of garlic, oil, oregano, and pepper flakes if you're using them.
2. Bring sauce to a simmer on med-high. Reduce heat to medium and keep the sauce at a steady, slow simmer for 40-45 minutes, till oil droplets float free from tomatoes.
3. While occasionally stirring, crush tomatoes on the side of the pot after 15 minutes have passed.
4. Remove pot from heat. Remove the onion. Using a fork, mash garlic cloves on the pot side. Smashed garlic should be thoroughly mixed into the sauce. Crush the tomatoes to your liking, season with salt, and serve warm.

Per Serving:

Calories: 241| Fat: 1g| Carbs: 3g| Sodium: 1098mg

☆ ☆ ☆ ☆ ☆

Shatta Sauce

Preparation Time: 10 minutes | Fermentation Duration: 10 days

Makes: 20 ounces

Ingredients:

- ½ cup lemon juice
- 2 garlic cloves
- 2 tablespoons tomato paste
- 3 ounces (about 14) dried Kashmiri or ancho peppers, stemmed
- 2 tablespoons non-iodized salt
- 1 tablespoon Aleppo chili powder
- 2½ cups non-chlorinated water
- 1 teaspoon granulated sugar

Directions:

1. Combine the garlic and chiles in a jar that has been thoroughly cleaned. To prepare the brine, combine the water and salt in a separate container and stir until the salt is dissolved.
2. The fermentation process should take around ten days, during which time the jar should be kept at ambient temperature and shielded from direct sunlight.
3. After the fermentation process is finished, strain the ferment and set aside a quarter cup of brine.
4. Mix the ferment, the reserved brine, the lemon juice, the tomato paste, the sugar, and the chili powder in a food processor or a blender. Blend until completely smooth.
5. The sauce can be kept in the fridge for up to a year.

Per Serving:

Calories: 100| Fat: 1g| Carbs: 1.7g| Sodium: 1103mg

☆ ☆ ☆ ☆ ☆

Papaya–Scotch Bonnet Sauce

Preparation Time: 10 minutes | Fermentation Duration: 10 days | Makes: 16 ounces

Ingredients:

- 2 ounces (about 9) fresh Scotch bonnet peppers, stemmed
- 2 tablespoons granulated sugar
- 2 ounces dried papaya, unsweetened
- 1 teaspoon allspice berries
- 2 garlic cloves
- 2 tablespoons non-iodized salt
- 2½ cups non-chlorinated water
- ⅔ cup lime juice
- ½ cup water

Directions:

1. Add the papaya, garlic, chilies, and allspice to a clean jar. The non-chlorinated water and salt should be combined separately in a separate vessel to form a brine.
2. If using a weight, place it on top of the jar before adding the brine, being sure to leave at least an inch of headroom.
3. The fermentation process should take around ten days, during which time the jar should be kept at ambient temperature, its lid tightly screwed on, and shielded from direct sunlight. It's important to burp the jar every day.
4. After the fermentation process is finished, strain the ferment while setting aside 9 tbsps. of the brine for later use. Combine the fermented sugar, brine that has been saved, lime juice, and water in a food processor or blender.
5. Blend the ingredients until they are completely smooth. The sauce can be kept in the refrigerator for up to a year.

Per Serving:

Calories: 212| Fat: 15g| Carbs: 1.7g| Sodium: 876mg

☆ ☆ ☆ ☆ ☆

Lacto-Fermented Sauce

Perp Time: 8 days | Servings: 6 cups

Ingredients:

- 2 cups spicy pepper rings (about 8 average size peppers)
- 3 crushed garlic cloves
- ½ tablespoon of fine sea salt
- 1 cup of filtered water

Directions:

1. Preparation is key - add the garlic and chili peppers to make a spicy and fragrant sauce. Stir the water with the sugar until it dissolves, then allow it to cool to room temperature before adding the salt. Use a pint-sized mason jar or something similar to hold all the ingredients for the brine.
2. Stir the brine daily or every two days, depending on the temperature of the room; it should take between two to three days to get hazy. Cover loosely with a lid and place in a cool, dark place away from direct sunshine for at least 24 hours before serving. To avoid mold growth on the surface, stir it at least once a day or every other day.
3. Process the tomato in a food processor until it is smooth and creamy, then put it in a glass jar and refrigerate it.

Per Serving:

Calories: 121| Fat: 1g| Carbs: 1g| Sodium: 1045mg

☆ ☆ ☆ ☆ ☆

Fajita Seasoning

Makes: 1 jar | Prep Time: 10 minutes

Ingredients:

- 1/4 cup Chili Powder
- 2 tbsps. Paprika
- 2 tbsps. Sea Salt
- 1 tbsp. Cumin Powder
- 1 tbsp. Garlic Powder
- 1 tbsp. Onion Powder
- 1 tsp. Cayenne Powder

Directions:

1. Mix all ingredients in a bowl until well combined. Store in an airtight container.
2. Use in place of store bough fajita seasoning packets for fajita meat. Season to your taste. You can also use it on veggies or salads to spice them up.

Per Serving:

Calories: 241| Fat: 1g| Carbs: 3g| Sodium: 567mg

☆ ☆ ☆ ☆ ☆

Homemade Chicken Gravy Mix

Makes: 1 Jar | Prep Time: 10 minutes

Ingredients:

- 3/4 cup sifted flour
- 3 tbsps. chicken bouillon powder
- 1 1/3 cups dry milk powder
- 1/4 tsp. ground sage
- 1/2 tsp. ground pepper
- 1/8 tsp. ground thyme
- 1/2 cup butter

Directions:

1. Combine all ingredients except for butter in a bowl, and stir to combine well.
2. Use a pastry blender to cut in butter until evenly distributed. Store in an airtight container in the refrigerator for up to 6 weeks.

Per Serving:

Calories: 354| Fat: 10g| Carbs: 15g| Sodium: 876mg

☆ ☆ ☆ ☆ ☆

Homemade Lemon Pepper Seasoning Mix

Preparation Time: 10 minutes | Makes: 1 Jar

Ingredients:

- 1/3 cup crushed pepper corns
- 1/4 cup kosher salt
- 5 large lemons

Directions:

1. Zest all the lemons and mix with crushed peppercorns in a bowl until well combined.
2. Line a cookie sheet with parchment paper and spread the lemon mixture evenly onto a baking sheet.
3. Bake in the oven on the lowest setting until the mixture is completely dry.
4. Add the dry lemon-pepper to a spice grinder and grind to desired texture.
5. Mix with the kosher salt and store in an airtight container for up to 3 months.

Per Serving:

Calories: 34| Fat: 1g| Carbs: 1.7g| Sodium: 345mg

☆ ☆ ☆ ☆ ☆

Satay Sauce

Preparation Time: 10 minutes | Makes: 1 Jar

Ingredients:

- 1 cup of unsalted peanuts, dry roasted
- 1/3 cup of water, filtered
- 1-2 minced garlic cloves
- 1/2 tsp. of soy sauce, dark
- 2 tsp. of oil, sesame
- 2 tbsp. of sugar, brown
- 1 & 1/2 tbsp. of soy sauce, light
- 1/2 tbsp. of lime juice, fresh if available
- 1/2 tsp. of pepper, cayenne, +/- as desired
- 1/3 cup of milk, coconut

Directions:

1. Place ingredients in a food processor or blender.
2. Process or blend till the sauce has a smooth texture. Taste and adjust if desired. Serve while warm.

Per Serving:

Calories: 36| Fat: 2g| Carbs: 2.7g| Sodium: 255mg

☆ ☆ ☆ ☆ ☆

Homemade Taco Seasoning Mix

Makes: 1 Jar | Prep Time: 5 minutes

Ingredients:

- 1 x 28-oz. can of tomatoes, whole, peeled
- 1 peeled, halved medium onion, yellow
- 2 large, peeled whole garlic cloves
- 2 tbsp. of oil, olive
- 1 tsp. of oregano, dried
- ½ tbs pepper flakes, red
- Kosher salt, as desired

Directions:

1. In a medium pan, combine tomatoes and their juice, onion, cloves of garlic, oil, oregano, and pepper flakes if you're using them.
2. Bring sauce to a simmer on med-high. Reduce heat to medium and keep the sauce at a steady, slow simmer for 40-45 minutes, till oil droplets float free from tomatoes.
3. While occasionally stirring, crush tomatoes on the side of the pot after 15 minutes have passed.
4. Remove pot from heat. Discard onion. Smash cloves of garlic on the pot side using a fork. Stir smashed garlic fully into the sauce. Crush the tomatoes as you prefer, season with salt, and serve warm.

Per Serving:

Calories: 241| Fat: 1g| Carbs: 3g| Sodium: 1098mg

☆ ☆ ☆ ☆ ☆

Italian Dressing Mix

Preparation Time: 10 minutes | Makes: 20 ounces

Ingredients:

- 1 tbsp. dried parsley
- 1 tbsp. onion powder
- 2 tsp. oregano
- 2 tsp. sea salt
- 1 1/2 tsp. garlic powder
- 1 tsp. pepper
- 1/2 tsp. dried celery flakes
- 1/4 tsp. thyme

Directions:

1. Mix all ingredients together and store them in an airtight container or jar.

Per Serving:

Calories: 140| Fat: 1g| Carbs: 10g| Sodium: 110mg

☆ ☆ ☆ ☆ ☆

Spicy Cajun Seasoning

Makes: 1 Jar | Prep Time: 5 minutes

Ingredients:

- 2 1/2 tsp. paprika
- 1 1/2 tsp. chili powder
- 1 tsp. salt
- 3/4 tsp. thyme
- 1/4 tsp. oregano
- 1/4 tsp. pepper
- 5 dashes of cayenne pepper

Directions:

2. Mix all ingredients together in a small bowl until well combined. Use immediately or store in an airtight container.
3. You can use this on veggies, meat, soups, or anything else that needs a Cajun kick.
4. You can also make it hotter by adding more cayenne pepper, or if you like, make it a little milder by reducing it.

Per Serving:

Calories: 241| Fat: 1g| Carbs: 3g| Sodium: 1245mg

☆ ☆ ☆ ☆ ☆

Ranch Dressing Mix

Preparation Time: 10 minutes | Makes: 20 ounces

Ingredients:

- 1/4 cup dried parsley leaf
- 1 tbsp. dried dill leaf
- 1/2 tsp. dried basil leaf
- 1 tbsp. garlic powder
- 1 tbsp. onion powder
- 1/2 tsp. ground black pepper

Directions:

1. In a small mixing bowl, combine all of the ingredients until well combined. Keep it in an airtight container.

Per Serving:

Calories: 100| Fat: 1g| Carbs: 1.7g| Sodium: 110mg

☆ ☆ ☆ ☆ ☆

Chile Infused Aperol

Yield: 2 servings | Cooking Time: 45 minutes

Ingredients:

- 6 ounces Aperol
- 1 halved small red Thai bird chile (including stem and seeds)

Directions:

2. In a glass, combine one halved small red Thai bird chile (with seeds and stem) and six ounces of Aperol. Allow it to stand for 10 minutes. Taste the mixture; if desired, allow it to stand for 5 more minutes for more heat. Strain into a small jar through the fine-mesh sieve.

3. DO AHEAD: You can make Chile-Infused Aperol 3 months in advance. Strain and chill with a cover.

Per Serving:

Calories: 90| Fat: 4g| Carbs: 6g| Protein: 22g

☆ ☆ ☆ ☆ ☆

Green Lacto-Fermented Hot Sauce with Nasturtium Leaves

Preparation Time: 15 minutes | Fermentation Duration: 3 wks. | Makes: 17 ounces

Ingredients:

- 6-8 cloves of garlic minced
- 3¾ cups finely minced assorted green peppers
- 1½ tablespoons sea salt
- 10-12 nasturtium leaves
- 2 tablespoons whey optional
- spring water

Directions:

1. Rinse the peppers. Take the stems and tops off the peppers. If you like your hot sauce on the milder side, remove the seeds and membranes from the pepper. Otherwise, leave it whole.
2. Use a food processor to mince the garlic, peppers, and nasturtium leaves. Fill a quart jar with the pepper mixture. Include sea salt, as well as whey, if used.
3. Fill the jar with spring water until there is only one inch of headroom left, then poke the mixture with a butter knife to ensure there are no remaining air pockets.
4. A fermentation weight should be placed on top of the mixture, and the quart jar should be covered with an airlock lid. Ferment for 2 to 3 weeks at room temperature.
5. After fermentation, you can blend it again to make it smoother and add more spring water if you want it to be more like a sauce. Put it in bottles, and then put it in the fridge.

Per Serving:

Calories: 260| Fat: 1g| Carbs: 27g| Sodium: 345mg

☆ ☆ ☆ ☆ ☆

Norwegian Hot Sauce

Preparation Time: 25 minutes | Makes: 1 Jar

Ingredients:

- 10-12 dried red chilies
- ¼ cup garlic, chopped finely
- ¼ cup dried ginger, chopped finely
- 1 cup hot water
- 2 tbsp. tomato puree
- ¾ tbsp. vinegar
- ½ tsp. cardamom
- 1 tsp. sugar
- 2 tbsp. shallots or onion, chopped finely
- ½ tsp. Szechuan pepper powder
- ½ tsp. black pepper powder
- ½ cup oil
- Salt to taste

Directions:

1. Place the dried red chilies in a bowl. Pour the 1 cup of hot water over it. Keep aside for 2-3 hours.
2. Strain the water and place the chilies in a blender along with ½ of the garlic and blend it. Add water if necessary.
3. Pour oil into a saucepan. Heat on a high flame. When the oil is well heated, reduce the flame and add the remaining garlic and ginger.
4. Sauté for a minute. Add the shallots.
5. Sauté. Add tomato puree, sugar and salt. Cook for 4-5 minutes.
6. Add the red chili paste. Keep stirring the mixture.
7. Add Szechuan pepper, black pepper powder, cardamom and vinegar. Mix well.
8. Simmer for a couple of minutes more.
9. When cool, transfer into a glass jar. Cover and refrigerate.

Per Serving:

Calories: 100| Fat: 1g| Carbs: 1.7g| Sodium: 1098mg

3.4: African Hot Sauce Recipes

Nigerian Pepper Sauce

Preparation Time: 10 minutes | Fermentation Duration: 14 days | Makes: 16 ounces

Ingredients:

- 2 tablespoons non-iodized salt
- 1 medium Roma tomato, halved
- 1 medium red bell pepper
- 2½ cups non-chlorinated water
- 1 teaspoon curry powder
- 8/10 ounce (about 3) fresh Scotch bonnet or habanero peppers, stemmed
- ½ red onion, halved
- 1 cube vegetable bouillon
- ¾ teaspoon salt (any kind)
- ½ cup olive oil for serving

Directions:

1. Combine the tomato, bell pepper, onion, and Scotch bonnet peppers in a jar that has been thoroughly cleaned. Create a brine by mixing the non-iodized salt with the water in a separate container.
2. After inserting a weight, if using, pour the brine into the jar, making sure to leave a headspace of at least an inch.
3. After firmly screwing on the lid, place the jar somewhere out of the direct light of the sun, where it can ferment for two weeks. It's important to burp the jar every day.
4. After the fermentation process is finished, strain the ferment and set aside 3/4 of a cup of brine.
5. Combine the ferment, the curry powder, the brine that was reserved, the bouillon cube, and the salt in a food processor or blender. Blend until a smooth consistency is achieved.
6. The sauce can be kept in the fridge for up to a year. Just before serving, combine one

Tunisian Harissa

Makes: 1 jar | Prep Time: 20 minutes

Ingredients:

- 6 dried red chilies
- 8 Guajillo chilies, medium-sized
- 4 tsp. red pepper, crushed
- 2 tsp. caraway seeds
- 1 tsp. fennel seeds
- Pinch of saffron (optional)
- 1 ½ tsp. coriander, powdered
- ½ tsp. turmeric powder
- 2 tsp. salt or to taste
- 4 sundried tomatoes, rehydrated
- 4 garlic cloves
- 2 tbsp. lemon juice
- 4 tbsp. olive oil

Directions:

1. Deseed the dried chilies and chop them with your kitchen scissors.
2. Place it in a bowl. Place your chilies in boiling water, cover them, then set aside for a while until softened.
3. Grind the crushed pepper, caraway seeds, fennel seeds and saffron in a food processor or blender until fine.
4. Add the softened red chilies without the water as well as Guajillo chilies, coriander powder, turmeric, salt, sundried tomatoes and garlic. Blend again.
5. Pulse while adding 1 tbsp. of olive oil at a time. Repeat until all the olive oil is added.
6. Grind until a smooth consistency is achieved.
7. Add lemon juice. If necessary, adjust the seasoning.
8. Transfer into a glass jar. Add olive oil over it to preserve it.
9. Keep it in the refrigerator. Will last for a

tablespoon of olive oil per one-fourth of a cup of pepper sauce.

Per Serving:

Calories: 260| Fat: 1g| Carbs: 27g| Sodium: 345mg

☆ ☆ ☆ ☆ ☆

month.

Per Serving:

Calories: 241| Fat: 1g| Carbs: 3g| Sodium: 567mg

Chapter 4
Hot Sauce Heat Levels

The spiciness of the fruits of the Capsicum genus, also known as bell peppers or hot peppers, is gauged using the Scoville scale. Its purpose was to figure out how much capsaicin was in different chili peppers. Capsaicin, an intriguing chemical, turns out to be the active component that produces heat in varying degrees.

One teaspoon of jalapeno pepper needs 4,999 teaspoons of sweetened water to reach the "no heat" level. In order to reduce the heat of a habanero chocolate pepper, 449,000 Scoville units are assigned.

Based on how much capsaicin a pepper (or spicy sauce) has, Scoville scale ratings are issued. According to some experts, transformation causes peppers to score too poorly when compared to the ratings provided by human tasters. In essence, it's an homage to Wilbur Scoville, the inventor of the chili heat scale.

Only four of the approximately 60 species in the Capsicum genus are grown in cultivation. Many of us are aware with the hot Padru00f3n pepper, which has 2,000 to 5,000 Scoville units (SHU). Depending on the brand, tabasco sauce contains between 100 and 50,000 SHU. Some peppers have no SHU ratings, no capsaicin, and no spiciness.

The Indian Army uses grenades made with the potent Indian Boot pepper to render its adversaries helpless.

Participants in the Super Spicy Pepper Eating Contest must consume 3-5 raw Reaper peppers, which have a Scoville heat rating of 7 to 11 million. The severity of the adverse effects increases as the scale moves up. While some people can withstand the heat, others like the SHU Pepper Zero world, which has no capsaicin. Always start out with a mild chili to establish a baseline if you're just getting started.

What is the world's spiciest chili pepper? Learn how hot the extract is compared to the extract. What are the many chili pepper varieties and their Scoville heat ratings? A list of peppers with their types and Scoville Heat Units can be found here.

Hot Pepper Heat Table:

Scoville Heat Units (SHUs)	Pepper & Extract Varieties	Type	Heat Rating
15,000,000 - 16,000,000	Pure Capsaicin	Super Hot	10
2,000,000 - 10,000,000	Pepper Extracts - i.e. The Source, Blair's Reserve	Super Hot	10
8,800,000 - 9,100,000	Norhydrocapsaicin	Super Hot	10
6,000,000 - 8,600,000	Homocapsaicin, Homodihydrocapsaicin	Super Hot	10
2,500,000 - 5,300,000	US Grade Police Pepper Spray	Super Hot	10
2,000,000 - 2,200,000	Carolina Reaper	Super Hot	10
1,500,000 - 2,000,000	Trinidad Scorpion, Butch T, Naga Viper, Common Pepper Spray	Super Hot	9
855,000 - 1,463,000	Ghost Pepper (Bhut Jolokia)	Super Hot	9
876,000 - 1,500,000+	Dorset Naga	Super Hot	7
350,000 - 855,000	Red Savina Habanero, Indian Tezpur	Hot	6
100,000 - 350,000	Habanero, Scotch Bonnet, Bird's Eye, Jamaican Yellow Mushroom	Medium	5
50,000 - 100,000	Thai Hot Peppers, Chilitepin, Santaka	Medium	4
30,000 - 49,999	Cayenne, Tabasco, Pequin, Aji Amarillo, Aji Charapita	Medium	3
15,000 - 29,999	Chile de Arbol, Manzano	Medium	3
5,000 - 14,999	Serrano, Yellow Wax Pepper	Mild	2
2,500 – 4,999	Jalapeno, Poblano, Chipotle Jalapeño, Mirasol	Mild	1
1,500 - 2,499	Sandia, Cascabella, NuMex Big Jim	Mild	1
1,000 – 1,499	Ancho Poblano, Anaheim, Pasilla, Espanola	Mild	1
99 - 999	Paprika, Mexican Bell, Pepperoncini, Cherry	Mild	1
0-99	Sweet Bell Peppers, Sweet Banana, Pimento	Mild	1

Chapter 5

Store Hot Sauce Long Term

Hot sauce is a staple in many kitchens, and it can be used to add spicy flavor to almost any dish. However, what happens when you run out of hot sauce? Can it be stored to use later, or does it need to be used right away? In this post, we will discuss how best to store hot sauce so that you can keep using it over the long term.

Storing Hot Sauce

Here's what you need to know about storing hot sauce long-term:

❖ Store in a cool, dry place. The ideal temperature range is between 50 and 70 degrees F (10°C - 21°C). A refrigerator or freezer is best for preserving the flavor and quality of hot sauces, but if you don't have either of these, store your bottles in a basement or wine cellar.

❖ Keep away from light. Hot sauces are sensitive to light and can become discolored if exposed to too much sunshine through bottle glass or clear plastic containers over time. You can mitigate this by keeping your hot sauces stored in opaque containers like mason jars or brown paper bags—or by choosing darkly tinted bottles like those designed with "green glass" on the label (for example, Death Wish Red Pepper Sauce).

❖ Keep away from heat and moisture. Heat can damage capsaicinoids (the compounds responsible for giving peppers their heat) as well as cause condensation inside the bottle that leads to bacterial growth; this is why refrigerating your bottle after opening it will help preserve its contents longer than leaving them out at room temperature where they may end up spoiling prematurely due to improper refrigeration techniques!

Short Term Storage

While you can store the hot sauce in the pantry, it's best to avoid direct sunlight, high temperatures and moisture. Hot sauce should be stored away from heat sources such as ovens or stoves. It is also best stored away from moisture, so don't keep it next to a sink or near your dishwasher.

Several options exist for short-term storage of hot sauce:

❖ Vacuum sealer bags will prevent air from coming into contact with your bottles. To use these bags properly, place several drops of water on both sides of the bag before sealing it shut and placing it in your freezer upright with some space between each bottle and its neighbors — this will help to prevent them from sticking together during freezing.* Glass bottles sealed with cork stoppers are another option for short term storage (these work especially well if you want to store hot sauce long term).

Long Term Storage

Store your hot sauce in a cool, dry place.

Do not store your hot sauce in the fridge. Chilling can affect the flavor of some sauces and make them taste bitter or dull. However, if you want to keep your sauce fresh for longer than a month or so, you can refrigerate it (but don't freeze it). Store any open bottles on their sides so that they don't leak onto other bottles — especially if you plan to keep them for more than six months!

Hot Sauce can be stored short and long-term.

Hot sauce can be stored short and long-term.

❖ Store in a cool, dark place — Like all other food items, the hot sauce should be kept away from direct sunlight and heat sources. If you have limited space in your kitchen, consider storing your hot sauce in the pantry or cupboard instead of on an open shelf or countertop.

❖ Store in a sealed container — A tightly sealed jar or bottle will keep out oxygen and moisture better than leaving it open to the air. You can also store them under refrigeration if you want to keep them fresh longer (though this isn't necessary).

As you can see, there are a lot of different ways that you can store your hot sauce. Whether it's short or long-term, the options are endless.

Chapter 6
Hot Sauce Dish

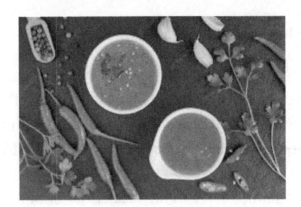

Chili Relleno Casserole

Serving Size: 4 | Preparation Time: 60 mins

Ingredients:

- 2 (10 ounce) cans of whole green chiles, drained
- 1-pound shredded Cheddar cheese
- 6 eggs
- 2 tablespoons all-purpose flour
- 1 1/2 (5 ounce) cans of evaporated milk
- 1-pound shredded Monterey Jack cheese
- 2 (15 ounce) cans of green enchilada sauce

Directions:

1. Preheat the oven to 200 degrees C (400 degrees F). Coat a 9x13-inch baking dish with grease.
2. To make a smoothie, mix evaporated milk, eggs, and flour in a mixing bowl. Place the remaining canned chiles on top of the Cheddar cheese. Spread the mixture over the cheese and chiles.
3. Take a casserole out of the oven and add green chili salsa and Monterey jack cheese. Bake for about 30 minutes in preheated oven until set, then put back into the oven for another 15 minutes.
4. Serve with enchilada sauce, and enjoy.

Per Serving:

Calories: 565| Fat: 34g| Carbs: 13.6g| Sodium: 1543g

Sos Ti-Malice Biscuits

Prep Time: 5 mis | Servings: 24

Ingredients:

- ½ ounce melted butter
- 4 ounces vegetable oil
- salt to taste
- ½ ounce Sos Ti-Malice
- 8 ounces of half-and-half cream
- 18 ounces of self-rising flour

Directions:

1. Preheat oven to 350 degrees Fahrenheit
2. In a bowl, combine flour, cream, oil, and Sos Ti-Malice; stir until a lumpy dough forms. It should be divided into two balls and baked for 15 minutes at 350 degrees Fahrenheit (200 degrees Celsius) or until golden brown.
3. Before serving, season the biscuits with salt and brush with melted butter.

Per Serving:

Calories: 150| Fat: 2g| Carbs: 50g| Protein: 6.2g| Sodium 456mg

☆ ☆ ☆ ☆ ☆

Cranberry Chutney Crostini

Serving: 2 dozen | Prep: 20mins | Cook: 20mins

Ingredients:

- 1 cup dried cranberries
- 1/3 cup chopped sweet red pepper
- 1/3 cup white wine vinegar
- 1/4 cup packed brown sugar
- 3 tablespoons chopped shallots
- 1 garlic clove, minced
- 1/2 teaspoon crushed red pepper flakes
- 1/4 teaspoon salt
- 1/4 teaspoon coarsely ground pepper
- 1/2 cup water, divided
- 1/4 cup chopped walnuts
- 24 slices French bread baguette (1/2 inch thick)
- 3 ounces cream cheese, softened
- 3/4 cup crumbled Gorgonzola cheese
- Minced chives, optional
- Salt to taste

Directions:

1. For chutney, put together the initial 9 ingredients in a big saucepan and add a quarter cup of water. Lower heat; allow to simmer without cover for 5 minutes. Add walnuts and the rest of the water; cover and allow to cook for 10 to 15 minutes.
2. Bake the bread on an ungreased baking sheet at 350° till browned lightly for 8 to 10 minutes. Scatter 1-1/2 teaspoons of the chutney over the top of each slice of bread and top with the remaining chutneys.

Per Serving:

Calories: 91| Fat: 3g| Carbs: 13g| Sodium: 162mg

☆ ☆ ☆ ☆ ☆

Chicken Bites With Lacto Fermented Serving

Serving: 2 dozen (1 cup sauce) | Prep: 25mins | Cook: 15mins

Ingredients:

- 1/2 cup buttermilk, divided
- 1-pound boneless skinless chicken breasts cut into 1-inch cubes
- 3/4 cup all-purpose flour
- 2 large eggs
- 2 cups crushed cornflakes
- 1/2 teaspoon onion powder
- 1/2 teaspoon garlic salt
- 1/4 teaspoon salt
- 1/4 teaspoon dried oregano
- Lacto-Fermented Sauce
- 1 cup apricot preserves
- 2 tablespoons prepared mustard

Directions:

1. Preheat oven to 350 degrees. In a shallow bowl, pour 1/4 cup of the buttermilk, then add the chicken. Mix together the oregano, salt, garlic salt, onion powder and cornflakes in a 3rd bowl. Whisk the leftover buttermilk and eggs in a separate shallow bowl.
2. Add the chicken to the flour and shake until coated. In a greased 15x10x1-inch baking pan, lay out the chicken. Dip the floured chicken into the egg mixture, followed by the cornflake mixture, then flip to coat.
3. Preparation is crucial - make sure the chicken is cooked thoroughly before adding the mustard and apricot preserves. Let it bake for 15 to 18 minutes or until the juices run clear, then serve it with Lacto-Fermented sauce and some extra-virgin olive oil.

Per Serving:

Calories: 102| Fat: 1g| Carbs: 18g| Protein: 1g| Sodium: 155mg

Fried egg sandwich with a touch of Momo's Chutney

Servings: 4 | Prep time: 10 minutes

Ingredients:

- 4 large eggs
- Salt, pepper
- 4 thick sourdough bread slices
- 4 slices Swiss cheese
- 4 large lettuce leaves
- 4 slices tomatoes
- 1 tbsp. Momo's Chutney or more
- Some butter or oil

Directions:

1. Line up all your ingredients on the kitchen counter.
2. Heat some oil or butter in the pan and fry your eggs without poking the egg yolk. Season with salt and pepper.
3. Meanwhile, toast the bread and butter it.
4. Add some fresh tomatoes, lettuce on top and then the cooked egg.
5. Finalize your meal by sprinkling some Momo's Chutney on top of your egg, using as much or as little as you like.
6. If you don't feel like cooking potatoes on some weekends, serve fried eggs on toast with Momo's Chutney.

Per Serving:

Calories: 215| Fat: 25g| Carbs: 15g| Protein: 18g| Sodium 1035mg

☆ ☆ ☆ ☆ ☆

Calzone Pinwheels

Serving: 16 appetizers | Prep: 20mins | Cook: 10mins mins

Ingredients:

- 1/2 cup shredded part-skim mozzarella cheese
- 1/2 cup part-skim ricotta cheese
- 1/2 cup diced pepperoni
- 1/4 cup grated Parmesan cheese
- 1/4 cup chopped fresh mushrooms
- 1/4 cup finely chopped green pepper
- 2 tablespoons finely chopped onion
- 1 teaspoon Italian seasoning
- 1/4 teaspoon salt
- 1 package (8 ounces) of refrigerated crescent rolls
- 1 jar (14 ounces) of pizza sauce, warmed
- Garlic And Achiote Fermented Hot Sauce

Directions:

1. Preheat the oven to 375 degrees. Mix the initial 9 ingredients in a small bowl.
2. Unroll crescent dough. Separate to 4 rectangles. Seal by pressing perforations. Spread cheese mixture within 1/4 in. of the rectangle's edges. Beginning with a short side, roll up like a jelly roll. Seal by pinching the seam.
3. Cut each roll into 4 slices by using a serrated knife. Put, cut side down, onto a greased baking sheet. Bake until golden brown or for 12-15 minutes. Serve alongside pizza sauce and Garlic And Achiote Fermented Hot Sauce.

Per Serving:

Calories: 118| Fat: 7g| Carbs: 9g| Sodium: 342mg

☆ ☆ ☆ ☆ ☆

Chicken and Shrimp

Prep Time: 10 mins | Cooking Time: 30 mins | Serves: 4

Ingredients:

- Chimichurri Sauce
- 2 tbsp cheddar cheese, grated
- 1 cup chicken, cut into small cubes
- 1 cup shrimp, cleaned
- 1 can (14 oz) navy beans
- 2 cups brown broth
- 1 cup coconut milk
- 1 tsp oregano
- 1/3 tsp paprika
- Salt and pepper to taste
- 1 tbsp butter
- 2 onions, chopped

Directions:

1. In a pot, melt the butter. Fry the chicken until golden.
2. Drain the navy beans.
3. Add the onions and fry until golden.
4. Add the beans, jalapeno pepper, shrimp, spices and seasonings.
5. Stir for 2 minutes. Pour in the brown broth.
6. Cook for 10 minutes. Add the coconut milk and cook for 5 minutes.
7. Serve hot with the cheddar cheese on top and Chimichurri Sauce.

Per Serving:

Calories: 200| Fat: 36g| Carbs: 8g| Protein: 67g| Sodium: 356mg

☆ ☆ ☆ ☆ ☆

Orange Satay Sauce shrimp

Prep Time: 15 mis | Servings: 6

Ingredients:

- 12 ounces frozen popcorn shrimp
- 2 ounces of orange marmalade
- 8.8 ounces basmati rice, cooked
- 4 ounces green onions, sliced and divided
- 1/4 teaspoon fresh ginger root, finely grated
- 1 ounce rice vinegar
- 1 teaspoon Satay Sauce
- 4 ounces of fresh orange juice
- ½ ounce soy sauce, low-sodium

Directions:

1. Preheat oven to 425 degrees Fahrenheit.
2. Line a baking sheet with aluminum foil and arrange the shrimp on the foil in a single layer. Cook shrimp according to the direction on the packaging.
3. Combine the rest of the ingredients except for the rice and half of the green onions in a saucepan on medium-high heat and bring to a boil. Cook for 1 minute and remove from heat.
4. Transfer the mixture in the pan to a large bowl and add the other half of the onions.
5. Cook rice according to the package instructions.
6. Stir shrimp into the sauce, Satay Sauce and serve over a bed of basmati rice.

Per Serving:

Calories: 340| Fat: 22g| Carbs: 29g| Protein: 13g| Sodium: 1242mg

☆ ☆ ☆ ☆ ☆

Buffalo Wing Poppers

Serving: 40 appetizers | Prep: 20mins | Cook: 20mins

Ingredients:

- 20 jalapeno peppers
- 1 package (8 ounces) of cream cheese, softened
- 1-1/2 cups shredded part-skim mozzarella cheese
- 1 cup diced cooked chicken
- 1/2 cup blue cheese salad dressing
- 1/2 Fermented Buffalo Sauce

Directions:

1. Lengthwise cut peppers in half; leave stems intact and discards seed. Mix leftover ingredients in a small bowl; stuff/pipe into the pepper halves.
2. Put into 15x10x1-in. greased baking pan and bake at 325°, uncovered, for 40 minutes for mild flavor, 30 minutes for medium or 20 minutes for a spicy flavor.

Per Serving:

Calories: 116| Fat: 8g| Carbs: 2.5 g| Protein: 6g| Sodium: 328mg

☆ ☆ ☆ ☆ ☆

Mexican Fiesta Platter

Serving: 20 servings | Prep: 15mins | Cook: 35mins

Ingredients:

- 2-1/2 pounds of ground beef
- 2 cans (16 ounces each) of kidney beans, rinsed and drained
- 2 cans (15 ounces each) of tomato sauce
- 1 envelope of chili seasoning
- 1 package (10-1/2 ounces) of corn chips
- 3 cups hot cooked rice
- 2 large onions, chopped
- 2 cups shredded Monterey Jack cheese
- 1 medium head of iceberg lettuce, shredded
- 4 medium tomatoes, chopped
- 1-1/2 cups chopped ripe olives
- Costa Rican–Style Hot Sauce

Directions:

1. Cook beef in a Dutch oven over medium heat until the beef is no longer pink, then drain. Put in chili seasoning, tomato sauce and beans; simmer, stirring occasionally, for about half an hour.
2. Layer the corn chips, the rice, the onions, the meat mixture, the cheese, the lettuce, the tomato and the olives on 2 serving platters with sides. Sprinkle the Costa Rican–Style Hot Sauce.

Per Serving:

Calories: 250| Fat: 18g| Carbs: 29g| Protein: 20g| Sodium: 645mg

☆ ☆ ☆ ☆ ☆

Thai Chinese Cabbage Salad

Serving Size: 5 | Preparation Time: 2 hrs. 20mins

Ingredients:

- 1 head Napa cabbage (also called Chinese cabbage)
- 1 tablespoon coarse salt
- 1 stalk of fresh lemongrass
- 1 large garlic clove
- 1 shallot
- Norwegian Hot Sauce
- 2 tablespoons fresh lime juice

Directions:

1. Remove outer cabbage leaves. Cut into 4 cabbage and core. Slice each quarter crosswise, 1/4-inch-thick. In a big bowl of cold water, rinse cabbage thoroughly, then spins it dry. Toss cabbage and salt together for 5 minutes till salt is dissolved in a big stainless-steel or glass bowl. In a colander set over a bowl, put cabbage. Drain cabbage for an hour. Wash cabbage thoroughly and press in small handfuls until completely dry. Meanwhile, trim the root end of the lemongrass and remove the outer leaves. Separately mince 2 inches of lemongrass, shallot, and garlic.
2. Toss lime juice, fish sauce, shallot, garlic, lemongrass, and cabbage in a big bowl. Salad can be done 2 hours in advance, put a cover and refrigerate. At cool room temperature, serve salad with Norwegian Hot Sauce.

Per Serving:

Calories: 26| Carbs: 5 g| Protein: 2 g| Fat: 0 g| Sodium: 423 mg| Fiber: 1 g

☆ ☆ ☆ ☆ ☆

Spicy Eggy Salad (Yum Kai Tom)

Yield: 3 servings | Cooking Time: 30 minutes

Ingredients:

- 6 pieces hard-boiled eggs
- 2 small shallots, chopped finely
- 2 tbsp. fish sauce
- 2 tbsp. freshly squeezed lime juice
- ½ tsp. dried chili flakes
- ½ tsp. palm sugar
- Indian-Style Chutney Sauce
- 2 sprigs of fresh cilantro

Directions:

1. Slice the hardboiled eggs into half. Set aside.
2. Prepare the salad dressing by mixing shallots with fish sauce, lime juice and sugar.
3. Stir continuously until the sugar is completely dissolved, and also stir in the chili flakes for some added kick.
4. Transfer the sliced eggs to a nice serving platter. Line the platter with fresh lettuce if desired. Drizzle the salad dressing over the eggs and top with chopped cilantro and Indian-Style Chutney Sauce.

Per Serving:

Calories: 161| Fat: 83.5g| Carbs: 11.3g| Protein: 12.2g

☆ ☆ ☆ ☆ ☆

Thai Waterfall Grilled Beef Salad (Nam Tok Neua)

Yield: 2 servings | Cooking Time: 45 minutes

Ingredients:

- 250 grams beef tenderloin
- ½ tsp. freshly ground pepper
- 2 tbsp. light soy sauce
- Salad dressing
- 2 tbsp. fish sauce
- ½ tsp. white sugar
- 2 tbsp. freshly squeezed lime juice
- 2 small shallots, minced
- 1 tbsp. toasted rice powder
- 2 tbsp. spring onion
- Kale Pesto Sauce
- Mint leaves for garnish

Directions:

1. In a bowl, mix the beef with freshly ground pepper and soy sauce. Marinate for at least one hour.
2. In a separate bowl, pour in the fish sauce, white sugar, lime juice and shallots. Mix well until the sugar is dissolved and set aside.
3. When the beef is fully marinated, prepare the grill. Grill the beef for about 5-8 minutes on each side or until medium rare. Be careful not to overcook the beef.
4. Allow the beef to cool for about 5 minutes. Slice into thin bite-sized strips.
5. Dump the beef strips into the bowl of dressing. Add in the toasted rice powder and spring onion. Mix thoroughly until every strip is coated with dressing.
6. Garnish with fresh mint leaves to give the salad a refreshing kick. Serve with sticky rice and a side of fresh lettuce leaves with Kale Pesto Sauce.

Per Serving:

Calories: 145| Fat: 4g| Carbs: 6g| Protein: 22g

Green Papaya Salad (Som Tam)

Serving: 2-3 | Cooking Time: 30 minutes

Ingredients:

- 2 cups of green papaya, julienned
- 4 cloves garlic, finely chopped
- Papaya–Scotch Bonnet Sauce
- 2 tbsp. brown sugar or palm sugar
- 2 tbsp. dried shrimps, coarsely chopped
- 3 tbsp. roasted peanuts
- 4 pieces long beans, cut into 1-inch size pieces (or substitute with 6 pieces green beans, blanched)
- 3 tbsp. fish sauce
- 1 medium lime

Directions:

1. Soak the papaya strips in ice-cold water for 10-15 minutes to make them crispier. Then drain it well and transfer it to a bowl.
2. Using a mortar and pestle, pound the garlic and palm sugar until it forms into a paste.
3. Then add in the long beans to the mortar and pound them as well. Add in the fish sauce and freshly squeezed lime juice. Make sure that the beans are thoroughly infused with all the flavors.
4. Add in the dried shrimps and peanuts. Add the coarsely chopped tomatoes as well and continue on pounding the mix.
5. Toss in the papaya and mix it well with the dressing.
6. Serve it with rice or as a side dish and Papaya–Scotch Bonnet Sauce

Per Serving:

Calories: 124| Fat: 3g| Carbs: 26g| Protein: 6g

☆ ☆ ☆ ☆ ☆

Chicken Pho

Yield: 3 servings | Cooking Time: 45 minutes

Ingredients:

- 2 thick slices (½ inch thick) of fresh ginger
- 2 quarts water
- 1 ¾ pounds chicken, quartered
- Honey-Jalapeño Sauce
- ¼ cup basil leaves, torn
- 1 tablespoon hoisin sauce, to serve
- 1 yellow onion unpeeled, quartered
- 1 teaspoon sugar
- ½ tablespoon salt
- 2 tablespoons Asian fish sauce
- ½ pound dried rice noodles
- 1 ½ pounds of chicken bones or chicken wings
- ½ pound bean sprouts
- 3 lime wedges
- 1 tablespoon Sriracha sauce or any other chili garlic sauce,

Directions:

1. Place onion and ginger on a baking sheet.
2. Roast in a preheated oven at 425° F for about 50-60 minutes or until brown.
3. Place a large stockpot over medium heat. Add bones, chicken, water, onion, ginger, salt and sugar into the stockpot. Bring to a boil.
4. Reduce heat to medium-low heat and simmer until chicken is tender.
5. Remove the chicken pieces and place them on a plate. Separate the meat from the bones and keep the meat in the refrigerator.
6. Add skin and bones into the soup pot. Simmer for another hour.
7. Now strain the broth and discard the solids.
8. Pour the broth back into the soup pot. Place on high heat and boil until the broth reduces to 6 cups. Add fish sauce and stir. Add the chicken meat and heat thoroughly. Meanwhile, add rice noodles into a bowl. Pour enough water to cover the noodles.

Phoritto (Pho + Burrito)

Servings: 4 | Cooking Time: 30 minutes

Ingredients:

- ½ tablespoon vegetable oil
- 2 jalapeño peppers, thinly sliced
- ½ pound frozen rib eye steak, thinly sliced
- 4 burrito- size flour tortillas
- 4 ounces of bean sprouts
- 1 medium onion, thinly sliced
- 1 can (14 ounces) beef flavored pho broth
- 5 ounces thin vermicelli style rice noodles
- 4 ounces of garlic chili sauce
- 1 tablespoon hoisin sauce or to taste
- ½ cup fresh cilantro, chopped
- ½ cup fresh Thai basil, torn
- Lime wedges to serve
- Chili Sauce and Tomatoes

Directions:

1. Place a saucepan over medium heat. Add oil. When the oil is heated, add onions and sauté until translucent.
2. Stir in the jalapeños and sauté until it turns dark green in color. Turn off the heat.
3. Pour broth into another saucepan. Place the saucepan over medium high heat. Add rib eye slices and cook until they are medium-rare. It should take 15-20 seconds. Cook in batches if required. Do not cook many in a batch.
4. Cook the noodles following the instructions on the package.
5. Warm the tortillas following the instructions on the package.
6. Spread the tortillas on a serving platter. Divide and spread the onion mixture on the tortillas.
7. Place rib eye slices and noodles over it. Drizzle some chili garlic sauce. Place bean sprouts. Drizzle some hoisin sauce. Sprinkle basil and cilantro.
8. Drizzle some of the broth mixture. Fold opposite sides of the tortillas over the

Let the noodles soak for 20-30 minutes or longer if necessary.

9. Place a large pot of water over medium heat. Bring to a boil. Add noodles and cook for a minute. Strain and divide the noodles into 3 serving bowls.

10. Divide and ladle the broth along with the chicken over the noodles.

11. Serve with bean sprouts, Honey-Jalapeño Sauce, basil, hoisin sauce and lime wedges.

Per Serving:

Calories: 145| Fat: 4g| Carbs: 6g| Protein: 22g

☆ ☆ ☆ ☆ ☆

filling. Roll to form a burrito.

9. Serve right away with lime wedges with Chili Sauce and Tomatoes.

Per Serving:

Calories: 124| Fat: 3g| Carbs: 26g| Protein: 6g

☆ ☆ ☆ ☆ ☆

Sweet and Sour Fish

Yield: 6 servings | Cooking Time: 55 minutes

Ingredients:

- 10 1/2 oz. fish fillet, sliced
- 2 tablespoons potato starch mixed with 2 tablespoons plain flour
- 1/3 cup cooking oil
- 1/4 cup green pepper, diced
- 4 shallots, peeled and halved
- 1/4 cup red pepper, diced
- 1/4 cup yellow pepper, diced
- 1 tomato, cut into wedges
- 1/4 cup pineapple, diced
- 1/2 cup ready or homemade Sweet and Sour sauce

For Sweet and Sour Sauce:

- 3 tablespoons chili sauce
- 5 tablespoons tomato sauce
- 3 tablespoons plum sauce
- 1 tablespoon lemon juice
- 2 tablespoons brown sugar
- 1 teaspoon salt

Directions:

1. Add all sauce ingredients to a pan and bring to a gentle boil. Turn off the heat and set aside.
2. Coat fish pieces in potato and cornstarch. Shake excess and set aside.
3. Heat a wok with oil over high heat. Fry fish in two batches. Deep fry until fish is crisp on the edges. Place on a rack. Heat for 15 seconds to make the oil hot. Add the fried fish slices back and fry till golden brown. Repeat with the second batch.
4. Leave 2 tablespoons of oil in a wok and pour out the rest. Heat over medium heat. Add peppers and onions in it. Fry for 1 minute.
5. Add tomato slices and stir fry for 20 seconds. Add diced pineapple and fry for a few more seconds.

Beef Lo Mein

Serving: 4 | Cooking Time: 30 minutes

Ingredients:

- 1/4 cup rice wine vinegar
- 1/2 cup oyster sauce
- 8 oz. Lo Mein noodles
- 1/4 cup soy sauce
- 1 1/2 lbs. flank steak, chilled
- 3 tablespoons honey
- 2 tablespoons + 1 teaspoon toasted sesame oil
- 2 large garlic cloves, finely chopped
- 1 1/2 teaspoons finely grated ginger
- 3 scallions, thinly sliced
- 1 medium red bell pepper, cut into 1/4 inch thick strips
- 8 oz. snow peas
- 1/2 teaspoon kosher salt
- Beurre Blanc Sauce

Directions:

1. Cook noodles in a pot with boiling salted water according to package instructions, and drain and rinse with cool water. Set aside.
2. Whisk soy sauce, oyster sauce, vinegar and honey in a bowl.
3. Slice beef against the grain very thinly. Transfer to a bowl, and toss with ½ teaspoon salt and ½ teaspoon pepper.
4. Heat 2 tablespoons of oil in a skillet over high heat.
5. Add beef and cook for 3 minutes, tossing often. Transfer to a plate.
6. Heat the remaining oil in the same skillet over high heat. Cook ginger, garlic and half of the scallions for 30 seconds while stirring.
7. Add bell pepper, peas and cook for 1 minute.
8. Add the oyster sauce mixture, reserved noodles and cook for 2 minutes, tossing occasionally.

9. Add beef and mix well.

6. Add ready or homemade sauce. Add 3 tablespoons of water to it. Stir quickly to mix well. Bring sauce to a boil.

7. Add fried fish slices to it and mix to coat well. Remove from heat. Once done, serves.

Per Serving:

Calories: 378| Fat: 4g| Carbs: 6g| Protein: 22g

☆ ☆ ☆ ☆ ☆

10. Divide among plates, top with scallions and Beurre Blanc Sauce, and serve.

Per Serving:

Calories: 124| Fat: 3g| Carbs: 26g| Protein: 6g

☆ ☆ ☆ ☆ ☆

Tomatoes with Hot Chicken

Total Prep Time: 30 minutes | Yield: 3 to 4 servings

Ingredients:

- Chicken boneless
- Onions chopped 2
- Tomato paste – 1 can
- Red chilies chopped – 1 cup
- Red chili sauce – 2 tablespoons
- Tomatoes 2
- Oil – 1 tablespoon
- Salt and pepper to taste
- Water hot
- Cumin powder 1/2 tablespoons

Directions:

1. Wash the chicken and cut it into small pieces. Take a pot and cook the chicken in it well.
2. Meanwhile, take the pan and put onions in it with salt and pepper.
3. Mix it well, take the onions out after cooking, and now add the tomato paste and tomatoes in it to make the paste.
4. Add cumin powder with red chili and red chili sauce, and add half a cup of hot water in it. Mix it thoroughly.
5. Now after the chicken is cooked, add the onions in the same pot as well as the tomato sauce. Cook it for about five more minutes and then serve.

Nutrition:

Calories: 50 calories; Carbs: 5.9 Protein: 2.7 Fat: 5.3

☆ ☆ ☆ ☆ ☆

Cider Sauce

Yield: 2 servings | Cooking Time: 45 minutes

Ingredients:

- 1 vanilla bean, halved lengthwise
- 1 pound Gala or McIntosh apples
- 2 cups unfiltered apple cider
- 1 stick (1/2 cup) unsalted butter, cut into pieces
- 1 small (1 1/2- to 2-inch) dried chile (preferably Thai)

Directions:

1. Use a sharp knife to scrape seeds from the vanilla beans into 2-3-quart heavy saucepan. Quarter the apples, but don't core or peel them. Add to vanilla seeds, including the pod and leftover ingredients; simmer, with no cover, for 1 hour.
2. Through a fine-mesh sieve, pass the sauce into the blender; don't press on the solids. Blend till emulsified. Be careful when processing hot liquids. Immediately serve.
3. You can simmer and strain the sauce, yet not blend. 1 day ahead; cover and chill. Reheat and blend barely prior to serving.

Per Serving:

Calories: 456| Fat: 4g| Carbs: 6g| Protein: 22g

☆ ☆ ☆ ☆ ☆

Caraway Coleslaw

Serving: 12 | Cooking Time: 5hrs

Ingredients:

- 1 cabbage head, shredded
- Pinch salt
- 1 tablespoon sugar

Dressing

- 2/3 cup low-fat mayonnaise
- 3 tablespoons cider vinegar
- 1/3 cup orange juice
- 2 teaspoons orange zest
- 2 tablespoons caraway seeds
- Salt and pepper to taste

Directions:

1. Place the shredded cabbage in a strainer.
2. Sprinkle with salt and sugar.
3. Stir to coat.
4. Let sit for 1 hour.
5. In a bowl, mix the mayo, cider vinegar, orange juice, orange zest, caraway seeds, salt and pepper.
6. Rinse the cabbage and drain well.
7. Transfer to a bowl.
8. Stir in the dressing.
9. Cover and refrigerate for 3 hours
10. Serve with Chile Infused Aperol.

Per Serving:

Calories: 165| Fat: 3g| Carbs: 26g| Protein: 6g

☆ ☆ ☆ ☆ ☆

Spiced Pumpkin Seed Flatbread

Yield: 2 servings | Cooking Time: 45 minutes

Ingredients:

- 1 cup lukewarm water (about 100°F.)
- 1 tablespoon sugar
- 1 teaspoon active dry yeast
- 3/4 stick (6 tablespoons) cold unsalted butter
- 2 1/2 cups all-purpose flour
- 1/3 cup cornmeal
- 1 tablespoon Spicy Southern-Style Barbecue Sauce
- 1 teaspoon table salt
- 1 cup hulled green pumpkin seeds(about 5 ounces)
- 1 large egg
- 2 tablespoons cold water
- coarse salt for sprinkling

Directions:

1. Stir yeast, sugar and lukewarm water together in a large bowl. Allow to stand for 5 minutes or until foamy. Cut the butter into bits. Mix with table salt, Spicy Southern-Style Barbecue Sauce cornmeal and flour into the yeast mixture, stirring just until a dough forms. Knead the dough on a lightly floured surface for 5 minutes or until they become smooth and the butter has incorporated. Shape the dough into a ball. Then place in the lightly oiled bowl, flipping it to coat. Cover in plastic wrap and let it chill for 60 minutes.
2. Start preheating the oven to 400°F, and flour two large baking sheets lightly.
3. Chop the pumpkin seeds. (The finer pumpkin seeds are chopped, the thinner flatbread will be.) Using a fork, beat cold water and egg together in a small bowl until they are combined well to create an egg wash. Split the dough in 1/2. Cover and

chill one portion. Roll out the remaining 1/2 dough, using a floured rolling pin, into a 1/8-inch-thick, rough oval on a lightly floured surface. Scatter 1/2 of the pumpkin seeds on top. Roll the dough as thinly as possible after pressing the pumpkin seeds into it with a rolling pin. Brush the dough with egg wash. Then cut into 6x1 inch long, thin wedges. Using a spatula, transfer the wedges to the baking sheets. Season with kosher salt to taste.

4. In the lower and upper thirds of the oven, bake the flatbread wedges for 10-15 minutes or until crisp, switching the sheets position halfway during baking. Let cool on the racks. With the chilled dough, create more flatbread wedges in the same manner. You can make flatbread wedges 3 days in advance; keep them at room temperature in an airtight container.

Per Serving:

Calories: 87| Fat: 4g| Carbs: 6g| Protein: 22g

☆ ☆ ☆ ☆ ☆

Spicy Rice With Shrimp And Peppers

Serving: 4 | Cooking Time: 30 minutes

Ingredients:

- 2 tablespoons extra-virgin olive oil
- 2 teaspoons plus 1 tablespoon of balsamic vinegar
- 4 green onions, chopped and divided
- 1-pound uncooked medium shrimp, peeled, deveined
- 1 tablespoon fresh lime juice
- 2 1/2 cups bottled clam juice
- 1/2 teaspoon annatto powder*
- 1/4 cup olive
- 1 cup chopped onion
- Salt and pepper to taste
- 1 garlic clove, chopped
- 2 plum tomatoes, seeded, chopped
- 2 tablespoons chopped fresh cilantro
- Pineapple Habanero Chili Sauce
- 1 cup medium-grain white rice

Directions:

1. In a small bowl, mix 2 tsp. of vinegar, 2 chopped green onions, and extra-virgin olive oil. Season the mixture with salt and pepper.
2. Toss the shrimp together with lime juice in a bowl. Allow it to stand for 30 minutes. In a small saucepan, boil the annatto powder and clam juice, stirring well until dissolved. Cover the bowl and put it aside.
3. Pour 1/4 cup of olive oil into a heavy large skillet and heat it over medium-high. Add the shrimp together with its accumulated juice into the pan. Sprinkle them with salt. Cook for 3 minutes until the center is opaque. Place the shrimp into a plate. Add the garlic, onion, 1 chopped green onion, tomatoes, and cilantro into the pan. Adjust the heat to medium. Cook for 3 minutes until the vegetables are almost tender. Pour

Steamed Red Snapper With Ginger, Chiles, And Sesame Oil

Yield: 2 servings | Cooking Time: 45 minutes

Ingredients:

- 1 (1-pound) red snapper fillet with skin (3/4 inch thick)
- 1 tablespoon medium-dry Sherry
- 1/2 teaspoon salt
- 2 tablespoons vegetable oil
- 1 (3-inch) piece fresh ginger, peeled and cut into 1/16-inch-thick matchsticks (1 1/2 inches long)
- 1 scallion, cut lengthwise into 1 1/2-inch-long very thin strips (1/3 cup)
- Louisiana Pepper Sauce
- 1/2 teaspoon Asian sesame oil

Directions:

1. Place a 9-inch steamer basket or metal cake rack in the deep 12-inch pan or a 12-14 inches wok (with the domed lid). Pour in enough water just to reach below the rack. Put on the wok cover and boil the water.
2. Score the skin of the fish several times. Place on a greased heatproof plate large enough to fit into a skillet or wok with a 1-inch clearance around the plate. Stir together the salt and Sherry in a small bowl, then rub both sides of the fish with the mixture, skin side up.
3. In a small skillet, heat vegetable oil over moderately high heat until it is hot but not smoking. Sauté scallion and ginger; stir for half a minute or until fragrant yet not brown, then scoop over fish. Place the fish (on a plate) carefully on the rack in wok; tightly cover. Steam for 7-8 minutes or just until the fish is cooked through. Take the plate out of the wok carefully. Sprinkle sesame oil over the fish and top with Louisiana Pepper Sauce.

in rice and 1 tbsp. of vinegar. Stir the mixture for 2 minutes. Pour in the clam juice mixture. Boil the rice mixture for 1 minute. Adjust the heat to low. Cover the pan and cook for 20 minutes until the broth has been absorbed and the rice is tender. Season the mixture with salt and pepper. Mix in the shrimp. Cover the pan and cook for 1 minute until the shrimp are heated through. Pour the mixture into a bowl and sprinkle it with chopped green onion. Serve this with dressing and Pineapple Habanero Chili Sauce.

Per Serving:

Calories: 124| Fat: 3g| Carbs: 26g| Protein: 6g

☆ ☆ ☆ ☆ ☆

Per Serving:

Calories: 382| Fat: 4g| Carbs: 6g| Protein: 22g

☆ ☆ ☆ ☆ ☆

Thai Chinese Cabbage Salad

Serving: 4 | Cooking Time: 30 minutes

Ingredients:

- 1 head Napa cabbage (also called Chinese cabbage)
- 1 tablespoon coarse salt and pepper
- 1 stalk of fresh lemongrass
- 1 large garlic clove
- 1 shallot
- La Jiao Jiang (Hot Chili Sauce)
- 2 tablespoons fresh lime juice

Directions:

1. Remove outer cabbage leaves. Cut into 4 cabbage and core. Slice each quarter crosswise, 1/4-inch-thick. In a big bowl of cold water, rinse cabbage thoroughly, then spins it dry. Toss cabbage and salt together for 5 minutes till salt is dissolved in a big stainless-steel or glass bowl. In a colander set over a bowl, put cabbage. After an hour, drain the cabbage. Wash cabbage thoroughly and press in small handfuls until completely dry. Meanwhile, while wearing rubber gloves, seed and mince the chiles. Remove the lemongrass's outer leaves and trim the root end. Separately mince 2 inches of lemongrass, shallot, and garlic.
2. Toss lime juice, fish sauce, shallot, garlic, lemongrass, and cabbage in a big bowl. Salad can be done 2 hours in advance, put a cover and refrigerate. At cool room temperature, serve salad, covered and chilled. Add La Jiao Jiang (Hot Chili Sauce)

Per Serving:

Calories: 24| Fat: 3g| Carbs: 26g| Protein: 6g

☆ ☆ ☆ ☆ ☆

Thai Roast Beef And Lettuce Rolls

Yield: 2 servings | Cooking Time: 45 minutes

Ingredients:

- 1/2 cup fresh lime juice
- 1/4 cup Asian fish sauce*
- 1/4 cup granulated or light brown sugar
- 2 large garlic cloves, minced
- 2 teaspoons Nuoc Cham
- 16 very thin slices of rare roast beef (3/4 to 1 lb)
- 16 large lettuce leaves, from 1 head Boston or 2 heads Bibb
- 16 fresh mint sprigs
- 16 fresh cilantro sprigs
- 2 carrots, cut into 1/8-inch-thick matchsticks

Directions:

1. In a medium bowl, whisk together Nuoc Cham, garlic, sugar, fish sauce and lime juice till the sugar is dissolved. Toss to coat roast beef with half of the sauce. Flavor with salt.
2. On a platter, arrange carrots, sprigs and leaves; serve with beef. Fill each lettuce leaf with some carrots, a cilantro sprig, a mint sprig and a slice of beef to assemble. Serve accompanied with the remaining sauce.

Per Serving:

Calories: 228| Fat: 4g| Carbs: 6g| Protein: 22g

☆ ☆ ☆ ☆ ☆

Zucchini With Garlic And Rhubarb Achar

Yield: 2 servings | Cooking Time: 45 minutes

Ingredients:

- Olive oil, 3 tablespoons
- 2 pounds of zucchini should be split in half lengthwise and then into 4 flat slices.
- Rhubarb Achar
- 4 minced garlic cloves
- table salt (preferably fleur de sel)
- 1 tablespoon freshly chopped parsley

Directions:

1. In a large, heavy skillet, heat the oil to medium-low. Add the zucchini and cook it for 5 minutes or until the slices are soft and lightly brown. Garlic should be added, and sea salt to taste when seasoning. Place the zucchini on the serving platter and garnish with the parsley and serve with Rhubarb Achar.

Per Serving:

Calories: 98| Fat: 4g| Carbs: 6g| Protein: 22g

☆ ☆ ☆ ☆ ☆

Yellow Tomato Soup

Serving: 4 | Cooking Time: 30 minutes

Ingredients:

- 1 large onion, chopped (about 2 1/2 cups)
- 6 bacon slices (about 5 ounces), chopped
- 5 cups chopped yellow tomatoes (about 2 pounds)
- 2 garlic cloves, minced
- 1/2 cup dry Sherry
- 1/2 cup dry white wine
- 4 cups chicken stock or canned low-salt chicken broth
- 2 teaspoons Flavorful Teriyaki Jerky
- 1 tablespoon freshly chopped oregano leaves
- 1/2 cup whipping cream

Directions:

1. In a heavy large pot, sauté bacon and onion over medium heat for 15 minutes or until the onion is starting to brown and tender. Put in garlic and tomatoes. Simmer for 20 minutes, stirring occasionally, until the tomatoes are juicy and tender. Put in wine and Sherry and simmer for 5 minutes. Put in stock, and simmer for 15 minutes or until the mixture is reduced to six and a half cups. Stir in oregano. In a blender, puree soup in batches. Put it back into the pot. Put in cream, then stir until they are heated through. Season with salt to taste. Then enjoy with Flavorful Teriyaki Jerky.

Per Serving:

Calories: 283| Fat: 3g| Carbs: 26g| Protein: 6g

☆ ☆ ☆ ☆ ☆

Hot Meatball

Preparation time: 10 minutes | Cooking time: 15 minutes | Servings: 4

Ingredients:

- 20 cooked meatballs, homemade or frozen
- 1 onion, halved and sliced
- 1 green bell pepper, cored and sliced
- 1 (16-ounce) can of red beans
- 1 (16-ounce) can of white beans
- 2 (14-ounce) cans of chili-seasoned tomato sauce
- 1 (10-ounce) can of mild tomatoes and green chilies
- Salt and pepper to taste

Direction s:

1. Combine all the fixings in a large saucepan over high heat. Stir well.
2. Let it boil; reduce heat to medium. Simmer within 15 minutes or until meatballs are heated thoroughly. Serve in shallow bowls.

Nutrition:

Calories: 246, Carbs: 29g, Fat: 4g, Protein: 19g.

☆ ☆ ☆ ☆ ☆

Blue Ribbon Chili

Preparation time: 10 minutes | Cooking time: 1 hour & 10 minutes | Servings: 8

Ingredients:

- 2 ½ cups tomato sauce
- 4 tbsp. chili seasoning mix
- 15 oz dark red kidney beans
- 2 pounds of ground beef
- ½ onion, chopped
- 1 (15 oz) can of light red kidney beans
- 1 tsp. ground black pepper
- 1 (8 ounces) jar of salsa
- Easy Marinara Sauce
- ½ tsp. garlic salt.

Directions:

1. Over medium heat settings in a large saucepan, combine your onions and beef; sauté until onion is tender and meat is browned, for 10 minutes. If desired, feel free to drain the grease.
2. Add in the seasoning mix, salsa, kidney beans, black pepper, garlic salt, and tomato sauce; mix well and decrease the heat to low and let simmer for a minimum period of an hour.
3. Serve with Easy Marinara Sauce.

Nutrition:

Calories: 456, Carbs: 28g, Fat: 17g, Protein: 51g.

☆ ☆ ☆ ☆ ☆

Hot Red Curry Chicken.

Preparation time: 20 minutes | Cooking time: 25 minutes | Servings: 6

Ingredients:

- 2 tbsp vegetable oil
- 1 lb. ground chicken
- 1/2 cup reduced-sodium chicken broth, divided
- 1 cup chopped sweet onion
- 1 tbsp. finely chopped garlic
- 1 tsp. grated fresh ginger
- 3 tbsps. red curry paste, divided
- 2 tsp. garam masala
- Homemade Lemon Pepper Seasoning Mix
- 1 tsp. salt
- 1 (13.5 oz.) can of coconut milk
- 1 (15 oz.) can of garbanzo beans, drained & rinsed
- 1 (14.5 oz.) can tomatoes, drained, diced
- 1 tbsp. cornstarch
- Chopped fresh cilantro (optional)
- Greek yogurt (optional)
- Warm naan bread (optional)

Directions:

1. Heat the oil in a big saucepan over medium-high heat. Cook until the ground chicken is no longer pink and crumbled, mixing from time to time, about 5 to 7 minutes. Remove from pan and set aside.
2. Turn heat to medium; put garlic, ginger, onion, and a quarter cup broth in a saucepan. Cook till the onion is soft, about 5 minutes, mixing from time to time.
3. Mix in salt, garam masala, and 2 tbsp curry paste; cook till spices are aromatic, 2 to 3 minutes longer. Mix in drained tomatoes, chickpeas, coconut milk, and cooked chicken. Let it boil.
4. In the meantime, in your small bowl, mix cornstarch and a leftover quarter cup of chicken broth. In a saucepan, mix in the cornstarch mixture.

Hot Tofu

Preparation time: 10 minutes | Cooking time: 1 hour & 5 minutes | Servings: 4

Ingredients:

- 2 tablespoons olive oil
- 1-pound extra-firm tofu, crumbled
- 1 medium onion, diced
- 1 green bell pepper, cored and diced
- 1 jalapeño pepper, minced
- 2 cloves garlic, minced
- 2 tablespoons chili powder
- 1 teaspoon cumin
- 1 (14-ounce) can of diced tomatoes
- 1 (14-ounce) can of tomato sauce
- 2 cups frozen corn
- 1 (16-ounce) can of black beans
- 2 cups water
- Banana Ketchup
- Salt and pepper to taste.

Directions:

1. In your large, heavy saucepan, combine olive oil plus tofu; sauté over medium-high heat for 1 minute. Add onion and garlic; sauté for 3 minutes.
2. Reduce heat to medium; add cumin, tomatoes, tomato sauce, corn, black beans, and water. Simmer for 1 hour, stirring often.
3. Remove from heat; add salt and pepper. Let stand for 5 minutes; serve with Banana Ketchup.

Nutrition:

Calories: 190, Carbs: 26g, Fat: 5g, Protein: 12g.

☆ ☆ ☆ ☆ ☆

5. Lower heat and let simmer until the mixture thickens, about 10 minutes. Take off the heat; mix in the leftover 1 tbsp curry paste.

6. Put yogurt, cilantro and Homemade Lemon Pepper Seasoning Mix on top of every serving, and if preferred, serve with naan bread.

Nutrition:

Calories: 334, Carbs: 28.3 g, Fat: 14.3 g, Protein: 23 g.

Hot Tomato Beef

Preparation time: 20 minutes | Cooking time: 60 minutes | Servings: 8

Ingredients:

- 1 pound ground beef
- 1 cup strong brewed coffee
- 4 garlic cloves, minced
- 1 (14.5 ounces) canned tomatoes with juice, peeled and diced
- ¾ pound spicy Italian sausage, casing removed
- 12 oz dark beer
- 6 oz tomato paste
- 1 tsp. ground coriander
- 2 onions, chopped
- 6 oz beef broth (14 ounces)
- ¼ cup brown sugar
- 1 tbsp. ground cumin
- 1 tsp. oregano, dried
- Beef Skirt with Chili Sauce
- 3 cans kidney beans (15 ounces)
- 1 tbsp. wasabi paste
- 4 tbsp. vegetable oil, divided
- 1 tsp. salt.

Directions:

1. Over medium heat settings in a large pot, put 2 tbsp of oil and cook the garlic together with onions, sausage, and beef for a couple of minutes, until meats are browned, stir well.
2. Add in the coffee, beer, tomato paste, tomatoes, and broth—season with sugar, cumin, coriander, oregano, wasabi, and salt.
3. Add in a can of beans, stir well and bring it to a boil; once boiling, decrease the heat, cover and let simmer.
4. Stir in the Beef Skirt with Chili Sauce and simmer for a couple of hours. Cook for 45 minutes more after adding the remaining two cans of beans.

Nutrition:

Calories: 250, Carbs: 36g, Fat: 4g, Protein: 16g.

☆ ☆ ☆ ☆ ☆

Hot Bean and Vegetable

Preparation time: 10 minutes | Cooking time: 27 minutes | Servings: 8

Ingredients:

- 3 tbsp. olive oil
- 1 large chopped onion
- 4 chopped celery stalks
- 3 minced garlic cloves
- 2 cups chopped mushrooms
- 1 tbsp. cumin
- 1 tbsp. chili powder
- Salt and pepper to taste
- 2 cups chopped tomatoes
- 2 cups fire-roasted tomatoes
- Joe's Soak Sauce
- 1 cup of vegetable broth
- 2/3 cup bulgur wheat
- 2 cups chili beans
- 2 cups pinto beans
- 3 tbsp. tomato paste.

Directions:

1. Heat the olive oil in your large pot. Sauté the onion, garlic, and mushrooms for 5 minutes. Stir in the spices, salt, and pepper and stir for 2 minutes.
2. Add the tomatoes, fire-roasted tomatoes, Joe's Soak Sauce, vegetable broth, beans, and tomato paste in a large mixing bowl. Stir well to combine. Simmer for 20 minutes.

Nutrition:

Calories: 112, Carbs: 22g, Fat: 1g, Protein: 5g.

☆ ☆ ☆ ☆ ☆

Hot California Green

Preparation time: 10 minutes | Cooking time: 40 minutes | Servings: 4

Ingredients:

- 6 cups fresh tomatillos
- Homemade Hot Sauce
- 1 cup chicken broth
- 1 teaspoon cumin
- 1/2 teaspoon oregano
- 4 cooked chicken breast halves, diced
- 1 green onion, minced
- 1/4 cup minced cilantro
- Salt and pepper to taste
- 1 ripe avocado, cut into thin wedges
- Sour cream, as you like.

Directions:

1. Place washed tomatillos in a large, deep saucepan. Cover with water; cook over medium-high heat for 30 minutes.
2. Drain tomatillos. Working in batches, place tomatillos and broth in a blender or food processor; purée.
3. Pour back into the saucepan. Add cumin, oregano, and chicken. Stir well; let it boil over medium-high heat. If the mixture seems too thick, add additional chicken broth.
4. Remove, then stir in green onion and cilantro. Add salt and pepper. Serve with wedges of avocado, Homemade Hot Sauce and sour cream for garnish.

Nutrition:

Calories: 110, Carbs: 10g, Fat: 6g, Protein: 3g.

☆ ☆ ☆ ☆ ☆

Lentil Chili

Preparation time: 10 minutes | Cooking time: 1 hour & 10 minutes | Servings: 12

Ingredients:

- 2 tbsp. olive oil
- 2 chopped onions
- 5 minced garlic cloves
- 2 cups dry lentils
- ¼ cup tomato paste
- 14 1/2 canned diced tomatoes
- 8 cups vegetable broth
- 3 tbsp. chili powder
- 1 tbsp cumin
- 1 dash Iran Pepper Hot Sauce
- Salt to taste
- 1 cup sliced carrots
- 1 cup (1 large) cubed potato
- 1 cup sliced mushrooms.

Direction s:

1. Heat the olive oil in a pot. Stir in the onions and garlic and sauté for 5 more minutes. Add the remaining **ingredients** except for the vegetables and Iran Pepper Hot Sauce and cover the pot.
2. Simmer for 40 minutes. Add the carrots, potatoes, and mushrooms and simmer for 20 minutes and serve with Iran Pepper Hot Sauce.

Nutrition:

Calories: 150, Carbs: 18g, Fat: 6g, Protein: 7g.

☆ ☆ ☆ ☆ ☆

Hot Pumpkin Turkey

Preparation time: 10 minutes | Cooking time: 20-25 minutes | Servings: 6

Ingredients:

- 1 tablespoon vegetable oil
- 2 cups pumpkin puree
- 1 cup chopped onion
- 1 1/2 tablespoons chili powder
- 1 dash salt
- 1 clove garlic, minced
- 1/2 cup shredded Cheddar cheese
- 1 pound ground turkey
- 1/2 cup sour cream
- Hollandaise Sauce
- 1 (14.5 ounces) can of diced tomatoes.

Directions:

1. Heat the oil in your large skillet over medium heat, and sauté the onion plus garlic until tender. Stir in the turkey, then cook until evenly brown.
2. Drain, and mix in the tomatoes plus pumpkin—season with chili powder, pepper, and salt. Adjust the heat to low, cover, and simmer within 20 minutes.
3. Serve with Hollandaise Sauce topped with Cheddar cheese plus sour cream.

Nutrition:

Calories: 285, Carbs: 14.9g, Fat: 16.6g, Protein: 21.2g.

☆ ☆ ☆ ☆ ☆

Clam

Preparation time: 10 minutes | Cooking time: 20 minutes | Servings: 4

Ingredients:

- 2 cups minced clams
- 1 cup clam juice
- 1 small onion, finely diced
- 1 green bell pepper, cored and diced
- 1 (14-ounce) can of small-diced tomatoes
- 1 (10-ounce) can of tomatoes and green chilies
- 1 (16-ounce) can of navy beans
- 1 cup heavy cream
- Instant-pot Ancho Chile Sauce
- Salt to taste.

Directions:

1. In a large, heavy saucepan, combine clams, clam juice, onion, chili powder, tomatoes, tomatoes, and green chilies. Bring to a boil over high heat.
2. Reduce heat to medium; stir in navy beans. Simmer for 20 minutes. Remove; stir in heavy cream, salt, and pepper. Serve with oyster crackers and Instant-pot Ancho Chile Sauce.

Nutrition:

Calories: 126, Carbs: 4g, Fat: 2g, Protein: 22g.

☆ ☆ ☆ ☆ ☆

Hot White Chicken

Preparation time: 10 minutes | Cooking time: 20 minutes | Servings: 4

Ingredients:

- 1 tablespoon vegetable oil
- 1 teaspoon dried oregano
- 1 onion, chopped
- 3 cloves garlic, crushed
- 2 (14.5 ounces) cans of chicken broth
- 3 cups chopped cooked chicken breast
- 1 (4 ounces) can of green chile peppers, diced
- 3 (15 ounces) cans of white beans
- 2 teaspoons ground cumin
- Spicy Coconut-Mint Chutney
- 1 cup shredded Monterey Jack cheese.

Directions:

1. Heat the oil in your large saucepan over medium-low heat. Cook, then stir the onion until tender. Stir in the garlic, green chile peppers, cumin, and oregano.
2. Stir the mixture until tender, within 3 minutes. Mix in the chicken broth, chicken, and white beans. Simmer for 15 minutes, stirring occasionally.
3. Remove the mixture from the heat. Slowly stir in the cheese until melted. Serve warm with Spicy Coconut-Mint Chutney.

Nutrition:

Calories: 684, Carbs: 74.9g, Fat: 0g, Protein: 59.1g.

☆ ☆ ☆ ☆ ☆

Hot Cheesy Taco

Preparation time: 10 minutes | Cooking time: 10 minutes | Servings: 5

Ingredients:

- 1 lb. ground beef
- 1/2 cup chopped onion
- 1 garlic clove, minced
- 1 can (16 oz.) kidney beans, rinsed and drained
- 2/3 cup cubed process cheese (Velveeta)
- 2 tbsps. salsa
- New Mexican–Style Hatch Green Chile Hot Sauce or Homemade Taco Seasoning Mix

Directions:

1. Over medium heat, cook the garlic, onion, plus beef in a broad saucepan until there is no pink beef left, then drain.
2. Put in the leftover **Ingredients**. Simmer without covering until the cheese has melted, about 5 minutes. Be sure not to boil. Serve with New Mexican–Style Hatch Green Chile Hot Sauce or Homemade Taco Seasoning Mix, and enjoy!

Nutrition:

Calories: 364, Carbs: 16g, Fat: 24g, Protein: 23g.

☆ ☆ ☆ ☆ ☆

Hot Mac and Cheese

Preparation time: 10 minutes | Cooking time: 20 minutes | Servings: 6

Ingredients:

- 1-pound lean ground beef
- 3 garlic cloves, minced
- 1 sweet onion, small to medium, diced
- 2 cups of Traditional Pasta Sauce
- 1 tablespoon extra-virgin olive oil
- 2 cups chicken broth, low-sodium
- ¼ cup parsley, fresh, chopped
- 1 teaspoon cumin
- ¾ cup Cheddar cheese, shredded
- 1 can tomatoes
- Ground black pepper and salt to taste
- 1 (16 oz) can of mild chili beans, undrained
- 1 ½ cups elbow macaroni, uncooked
- Turmeric Jerk Sauce

Directions:

1. Heat the olive oil over medium-high heat settings in a large-sized pot or Dutch oven.
2. Once hot, add in the garlic, onion, and beef. Cook within a couple of minutes until the meat is nicely browned and crumbly, stirring frequently; drain any excess fat.
3. Stir in beans, diced tomatoes, Pasta sauce, chicken broth, cumin, and chili powder—season with pepper and salt to taste.
4. Let the mixture boil over moderate heat settings and then stir in the pasta; cover and decrease the heat settings and let simmer for 12 to 15 minutes, until pasta is al dente.
5. Remove the pot from heat. Add in the cheese and parsley; stir well. Feel free to garnish it with more cheese and parsley; serve hot with Turmeric Jerk Sauce, and enjoy!

Nutrition:

Calories: 270, Carbs: 24g, Fat: 17g, Protein: 8g.

☆ ☆ ☆ ☆ ☆

Hot Lemony Chorizo Chicken

Preparation time: 10 minutes | Cooking time: 2 hours & 15 minutes | Servings: 6

Ingredients:

For the Chili:

- 28 ounce can of fire-roasted tomatoes, diced with juice
- ½ - 1 can of tomato paste (6 ounces)
- 1 onion, medium, chopped
- 2 pounds chicken thighs, boneless, trimmed, and cubed
- 1 can of each white kidney bean and red kidney
- 15 oz beans, drained and rinsed
- ½ heaping tablespoon of brown sugar
- 1 tablespoon chili powder
- 1 red bell pepper, chopped
- ¾ pound chorizo sausage, casings removed
- 3 garlic cloves, finely chopped
- 1 tablespoon cumin
- ½ tablespoon cocoa, unsweetened
- 3 cups chicken broth
- ½ tablespoon olive oil
- Salt to taste.

For Lime-Cilantro Sour Cream:

- 2 tablespoons lime juice, fresh
- ½ cup sour cream
- 1 tablespoon cilantro, fresh, chopped
- ½ tablespoon lime zest, finely grated
- Salt to taste.

For Serving:

- Fritos
- Lime wedges
- Fresh cilantro
- Cheddar cheese
- Avocado.
- Romesco Sauce

Hot With Baked Beans

Preparation time: 15 minutes | Cooking time: 10 minutes | Servings: 8

Ingredients:

- 2 cups water
- 1 medium onion, chopped
- 2 celery ribs, chopped
- 1 medium carrot, chopped
- 3 cups Stovetop Baked Beans
- 2 cans (14-1/2 oz. each) of diced tomatoes, undrained
- Salt to taste
- 1 dash of Tunisian Harissa

Directions:

1. Boil the carrot, celery, onion, and water in a big saucepan. Lower heat and simmer for 8-10 minutes, uncovered, until veggies are crisp-tender.
2. Mix in the remaining ingredients and heat through. Serve with Tunisian Harissa, and enjoy!

Nutrition:

Calories: 260, Carbs: 33g, Fat: 7g, Protein: 16g.

☆ ☆ ☆ ☆ ☆

Directions:

1. In a small-sized bowl, mix chili powder with brown sugar, cumin, and unsweetened cocoa; set aside.
2. Over medium-high heat settings in a large pot or a Dutch oven, heat the olive oil; stir and cook the chorizo in hot oil until heated through for 3 to 5 minutes.
3. Using a large, slotted spoon, remove the chorizo from a bowl. Season the chicken with pepper and salt and then add to the oil; brown all sides of the meat for 4 to 5 minutes.
4. Add the chicken to the bowl with the chorizo using the same slotted spoon. Add pepper and onion to the pan; sauté until beginning to soften, for a couple of minutes.
5. Add in the chopped garlic; sauté for one more minute. Add the mixed spices to the garlic, pepper, onion mixture, and sauté for more minutes.
6. Add in fire-roasted tomatoes, the chicken broth, and meat, scraping down the bottom of the pan to loosen bits and pieces.
7. Bring the mixture to a boil. Once boiling, decrease the heat settings and let simmer until chicken is tender and easily falls apart, uncovered for 1 and ½ to 2 hours.
8. Add ½ can of tomato paste and beans to the pot. Feel free to adjust the quantity of tomato paste. Now, mix all the sour cream in a large bowl; mix well for the sour cream. Serve with Romesco Sauce and enjoy!

Nutrition:

Calories: 260, Carbs: 30g, Fat: 8g, Protein: 18g.

☆ ☆ ☆ ☆ ☆

Hot Dog

Preparation time: 10 minutes | Cooking time: 20 minutes | Servings: 6

Ingredients:

- ½ can tomato sauce (10 ounces)
- 1 pound ground beef
- 2 ½ teaspoons chili powder
- ½ cup ketchup
- ½ teaspoon of each onion powder and white sugar
- 1/3 cup water
- 1 dash of ZHUG
- ½ tsp of each ground black pepper & salt.

Direction s:

1. In a large-sized saucepan, place the ground beef with water. Using a potato masher, mash the beef to break it apart.
2. Add onion powder, tomato sauce, chili powder, black pepper, ketchup, sugar, and salt; stir well and let the mixture boil over moderate heat settings.
3. Once boiling, switch to medium and cook for 15 to 20 minutes, until the beef is completely cooked, and the chili has slightly thickened.
4. Serve with ZHUG for a spicy taste.

Nutrition:

Calories: 100, Carbs: 7g, Fat: 6g, Protein: 5g.

☆ ☆ ☆ ☆ ☆

Hot Casablanca

Preparation time: 10 minutes | Cooking time: 15-20 minutes | Servings: 6

Ingredients:

- 3 cups cooked ham, cut into one-inch cubes
- 2 tbsps. brown sugar
- 1 tsp. ground allspice
- 1 (9 oz.) package of mango chutney
- 2 tbsps. lime juice
- 2 tbsps. creamy peanut butter
- 1/4 cup raisins
- 1 (15 oz.) can of chickpeas, rinsed & drained
- 1 (16 oz.) can of chili beans in spicy sauce
- 2 (10 oz.) cans of tomatoes with green
- Ranch Dressing Mix

Directions:

1. Mix diced tomatoes, chili beans, chickpeas, raisins, peanut butter, lime juice, mango chutney, allspice, brown sugar, and cubed ham in a large saucepan (or a Dutch oven).
2. Cook on medium-high heat, often stirring, until thoroughly heated for about 15 to 20 minutes.
3. Serve with Ranch Dressing Mix.

Nutrition:

Calories: 610, Carbs: 90.3 g, Fat: 17.6 g, Protein: 28.2 g.

Hot Butternut Squash

Preparation time: 10 minutes | Cooking time: 60 minutes | Servings: 6

Ingredients:

- 3 tablespoons tomato paste
- 1 pound ground turkey, 99% fat-free
- 4 plum tomatoes, ripe, chopped
- 1 onion, medium, diced
- 3 garlic cloves, minced
- ¼ cup sour cream, reduced-fat
- 1 tablespoon ground cumin
- ¼ cup chili powder
- 2 (14 oz each) cans of black beans, drained and rinsed
- 1 butternut squash, small, peeled, seeded, and cut into ½" cubes
- 2 teaspoons ground coriander
- ¼ cup cilantro leaves, fresh, chopped
- ¼ cup chia seeds
- Kosher salt to taste
- 3 teaspoons olive oil
- Fermented Thai-Style Green Curry Sauce.

Directions:

1. Over medium-high heat settings in a large Dutch oven, heat 1 and ½ teaspoons of oil.
2. Once hot, add in the turkey; cook for 4 to 5 minutes, until nicely browned, don't forget to break up the chunks using the side of a large wooden spoon.
3. Leave the center of the pan empty and push the turkey to the edges. Decrease the heat to medium and then add in the leftover 1 and ½ teaspoons of oil, then the garlic and onion to the middle of the pan.
4. Cook for 3 to 5 minutes, until the vegetables, begin to soften, stirring now and then.
5. Add in the cumin, chili powder, and coriander; stir well for half a minute. Add in the tomato paste and 1 teaspoon of salt; stir for half a minute until the paste turns to darken in color.

6. Add in the tomatoes, squash, and 4 cups of water.
7. Bring everything to a simmer for half an hour or a little longer until the squash is tender and the chili is thickened and uncovered.
8. Stir the chia seeds and beans well and heat through for 3 to 5 minutes, add salt.
9. Spoon the fermented Thai-style green curry sauce into separate large bowls and top each bowl with a dollop of sour cream and fresh cilantro.

Nutrition:

Calories: 164, Carbs: 21g, Fat: 3g, Protein: 13g.

Hot Pumpkin

Preparation time: 10 minutes | Cooking time: 1 hour & 15 minutes | Servings: 10

Ingredients:

- 1 can pumpkin purée (29 ounces)
- 6 small links of chicken maple sausage, thinly sliced (9 ounces); reserve with the ground turkey
- 1 (15.5 oz) can of red kidney beans
- 1 ½ pounds extra lean ground turkey
- 1 can diced tomatoes (28 ounces)
- 1 sweet onion, chopped
- 3 garlic cloves, minced
- 1 (15.5 ounces) can of cannellini beans, drained & rinsed
- 1 yellow and orange bell pepper, diced
- ½ cup chicken broth
- 2 tablespoon chili powder
- 1 teaspoon oregano
- 2 teaspoon brown sugar
- 1 bottle of pumpkin beer (12 fluid ounces)
- 4 tablespoon olive oil
- 1 teaspoon cumin
- Pepper and sea salt to taste.

For garnish:

- Green onions, sliced
- Texas-Style Picante Sauce
- Cheddar cheese, grated.

Directions:

1. Over moderate heat in a large-sized heavy-bottomed pot, heat 2 tablespoons of olive oil.
2. Once hot, sauté the onion and the garlic for a couple of minutes until translucent. Then sauté the bell peppers for 3 to 5 minutes; set aside.
3. Add 2 tablespoons of olive oil to the same pot, and brown the sausage and ground turkey for 8 to 10 minutes—season with sea salt.
4. Put the vegetables back in the pot once the

Hot Quinoa

Preparation time: 10 minutes | Cooking time: 45 minutes | Servings: 6

Ingredients:

- 1 cup quinoa
- 2 cups vegetable broth
- 1 tbsp. olive oil
- 1 chopped onion
- 3 minced garlic cloves
- 1 tbsp. chili powder
- 1 tsp. cumin
- ½ tsp. marjoram
- 1 cup tomato sauce
- 2 cans drained chili beans
- 1 diced green bell pepper
- 1 cup sliced mushrooms
- Chipotle Pepper Oil
- 1 cup of vegetable broth.

Directions:

1. Add the vegetable broth and quinoa to a pan. Bring to a boil, then bring to a boil. Adjust the heat to simmer, then cook for 20 minutes. The broth should be absorbed.
2. Heat the olive oil in a pot. Sauté the onion plus garlic within 5 minutes. Stir in the spices and add the remaining **ingredients** except for the cooked quinoa.
3. Simmer for 20 minutes. Add the quinoa and simmer for 5 minutes. Serve and enjoy!

Nutrition:

Calories: 140, Carbs: 25g, Fat: 2g, Protein: 5g.

☆ ☆ ☆ ☆ ☆

meat is browned, then add in the diced tomatoes, beans, pumpkin, and spices.

5. Add in the chicken broth and pumpkin beer; stir to combine.

6. Adjust the heat to low and simmer for a couple of hours, stirring now and then. Taste and adjust the amount of pepper and salt to taste, if necessary.

7. Serve warm with some sliced green onions, some grated cheddar cheese, and a Texas-Style Picante Sauce.

Nutrition:

Calories: 412, Carbs: 39g, Fat: 16g, Protein: 31g.

☆ ☆ ☆ ☆ ☆

Hot Smoky Vegan

Preparation time: 10 minutes | Cooking time: 25 minutes | Servings: 8

Ingredients:

- 2 tsp. olive oil
- 1 onion, chopped
- 1 (12 oz.) package of vegetarian burger crumbles
- 1 tsp. browning sauce
- 2 (15 oz.) cans of stewed tomatoes
- 2 cups vegetable broth
- 1 (15 oz.) can of chili beans
- 1 (15 oz.) can of tomato sauce
- 1 (6 oz.) can of tomato paste
- Cantaloupe Chutney
- 1 tsp. salt, or more to taste.

Directions:

1. In a big pot, heat olive oil on medium heat. Sauté onion in hot oil for 5 minutes until tender.
2. Mix in browning sauce, and burger crumbles until sauce coats onion and crumbles. Add salt, tomato paste, tomato sauce, chili beans, vegetable broth, and stewed tomatoes.
3. Once the mixture begins to boil, lower the heat to medium-low. Cook for 15-20 minutes or until the beans and tomatoes are soft.
4. Serve with Cantaloupe Chutney, and enjoy.

Nutrition:

Calories: 194, Carbs: 29.9 g, Fat: 4.1 g, Protein: 13.7 g.

☆ ☆ ☆ ☆ ☆

Hot Buffalo Chicken

Preparation time: 15 minutes | Cooking time: 1 hour & 15 minutes | Servings: 10

Ingredients:

- 1 tbsp. extra-virgin olive oil
- 2 tbsp butter
- 2 lbs. ground chicken breast
- 1 large carrot, peeled and finely chopped
- 1 large onion, chopped
- 3 stalks of celery, finely chopped
- 5 cloves garlic, chopped
- 5 tbsp chili powder
- 2 tbsp ground cumin
- 1 tbsp ground paprika
- salt and pepper to taste
- 1/2 Fermented Buffalo Sauce
- 2 (15 oz.) cans of tomato sauce
- 1 (15 oz.) can of crushed tomatoes
- 1 (15 oz.) can of white kidney, drained
- 1 (19 oz.) can of red kidney beans, drained.

Directions:

1. In a large pot, warm butter and olive oil over medium-high heat. Cook and stir chicken for 7-10 minutes, until the chicken is no longer pinkish.
2. Mix in celery, salt, pepper, chili powder, carrot, cumin, garlic, paprika, and onion. Allow it to cook within 3-4 minutes until the vegetables start to tender and the onion is already translucent.
3. Add tomato sauce, white and red kidney beans, hot sauce, and crushed tomatoes into the mixture. Allow it to boil.
4. Adjust the heat to medium-low and bring the mixture to a simmer for 1 hour. Serve and enjoy!

Nutrition:

Calories: 301, Carbs: 30 g, Fat: 8.6 g, Protein: 28.3 g.

☆ ☆ ☆ ☆ ☆

Hot Bread Bowl

Preparation time: 10 minutes | Cooking time: 30 minutes | Servings: 12

Ingredients:

- 1/2 lb. ground beef
- 1/2 lb. ground pork
- 2 cans (16 oz. each) of kidney beans, rinsed & drained
- 2 cans (14-1/2 oz. each) diced tomatoes with garlic and onion, undrained
- 1 can (14-1/2 oz.) beef broth
- 1 can (8 oz.) tomato sauce
- 2 tbsps. chili powder
- 12 hard rolls (about 4-1/2 inches), optional
- Optional:
- Shredded cheddar cheese
- Sliced green onions
- Canned Mexican Hot Sauce.

Directions:

1. Cook pork and beef in a big saucepan over medium heat until they are not pink; drain.
2. Mix chili powder, tomato sauce, broth, tomatoes, and beans. Heat to a boil. Lower heat, and allow to simmer for 20 minutes, while covered.
3. Place into soup bowls to serve or, if wished, slice the top fourth off of each roll, then carefully make a hollow from the bottom, save a 1/2-inch shell.
4. Cut removed bread into cubes. Spoon chili into bread bowls. If desired, serve with Canned Mexican Hot Sauce, sliced green onions, shredded cheddar cheese, and cubed bread.

Nutrition:

Calories: 292, Carbs: 40 g, Fat: 8 g, Protein: 16 g.

☆ ☆ ☆ ☆ ☆

Mexican Corn

Preparation time: 4 minutes | Cooking time: 30 minutes | Servings: 4

Ingredients:

- 4 sweet corn ears, husks removed
- 2 tablespoons olive oil
- Salt to taste
- 1 tablespoon olive oil
- ¼ cup breadcrumbs
- ½ teaspoon smoked paprika
- ½ teaspoon dried Mexican oregano
- 4 oz. cream cheese
- ¼ sour cream
- 2 tablespoons lime juice
- 2 crispy bacon slices, crumbled
- Fresh cilantro, chopped
- Lime wedges
- Canned Mexican Hot Sauce.

Directions:

1. Brush the corn with 2 tablespoons of olive oil.
2. Grill over medium high heat for 10 minutes, turning occasionally.
3. Season the grilled corn with salt.
4. Add the remaining oil to a pan over medium heat.
5. Cook the breadcrumbs until browned.
6. Stir in the oregano and paprika.
7. Cook for 30 seconds, stirring often.
8. Mix the cream cheese, sour cream and lime juice.
9. Spread the mixture on all sides of the corn.
10. Sprinkle with the breadcrumbs, crumbled bacon, cilantro and Mexican hot sauce
11. Garnish with lime wedges.

Nutrition:

Calories: 292, Carbs: 40 g, Fat: 8 g, Protein: 16 g.

☆ ☆ ☆ ☆ ☆

Italian Spaghetti Salad

Preparation time: 10 minutes | Cooking time: 3hrs | Servings: 15

Ingredients:

- 16 oz. spaghetti noodles, broken in half
- 1 green pepper, chopped
- 1 sweet red pepper, chopped
- 3 tomatoes, diced
- 1 cucumber, diced
- 3 zucchini, diced
- 8 oz. Italian salad dressing
- 1 ½ teaspoons poppy seeds
- 1 ½ teaspoons sesame seeds
- 1/8 teaspoon garlic powder
- ¼ teaspoon celery seed
- ½ teaspoon paprika
- 2 tablespoons Parmesan cheese, grated
- Hot and orange dressing.

Directions:

1. Prepare the spaghetti according to the directions in the package.
2. Rinse and drain.
3. Transfer the spaghetti to a bowl.
4. Stir in the green pepper, sweet red pepper, tomatoes, cucumber and zucchini.
5. In another bowl, mix the Italian salad dressing, poppy seeds, sesame seeds, garlic powder, celery sweet, paprika and Parmesan cheese.
6. Pour the mixture over the pasta salad and toss to coat evenly with the dressing.
7. Cover the bowl.
8. Refrigerate for 2 hours before serving with Hot and orange dressing.

Nutrition:

Calories: 292, Carbs: 40 g, Fat: 8 g, Protein: 16 g.

☆ ☆ ☆ ☆ ☆

Final Words

All in all, this book is a highly enjoyable compilation of recipes that are well worth trying out. The ingredients are fairly common, but they still bring together a great variety of meals that can be prepared in a wide variety of settings. Sure, it's no secret that hot sauce goes well with many foods, and some gourmet hot sauce even comes marketed with an assortment of delicious recipes. But what possesses someone to collect recipes from around the world and compile them with such an efficient use of space? For that matter, why would one think to make pineapple salsa or avocado hot sauce? The Worldwide Hot Sauce Cookbook successfully answers these questions and more, and although it is not going to change your life by any means, it will provide you with plenty of interesting meals for a long time to come.

The recipes featured in this book come from all over the world. The hot sauces featured vary in flavor, so there is sure to be something for everyone. Each sauce is unique in its own way, but its spicy kick ties them all together.

I hope you enjoy this collection of recipes that can add a little something to your meal. The Hot Sauce World offers many more serious and fun sauces to try from around the world, but this is a great starting point for anyone looking to expand their repertoire.

Made in United States
Orlando, FL
13 November 2023